AF773958

POLITICAL ECONOMY IN NINETEENTH-CENTURY AMERICA

Selected and Introduced by
Morgen Witzel

Volume 3

History of American Thought

Political Economy in Nineteenth-Century America

Selected and Introduced by **Morgen Witzel**

Volume 1
Mathew Carey
Essays on Political Economy, 1822

Volume 2
Francis Wayland
The Elements of Political Economy, 1837

Volume 3
George Tucker
Political Economy for the People, 1859

Volume 4
Amasa Walker
The Science of Wealth: A Manual of Political Economy, 1866

Volume 5
William Graham Sumner
Problems in Political Economy, 1884 and
Essays on Political Economy, 1885

Volume 6
Francis A. Walker
Political Economy, 1892

Printed in England by Antony Rowe Ltd, Chippenham

POLITICAL ECONOMY FOR THE PEOPLE

George Tucker

THOEMMES PRESS

Published by Thoemmes Press, 2003

Thoemmes Press
11 Great George Street
Bristol BS1 5RR, England

http://www.thoemmes.com

Political Economy in Nineteenth-Century America
6 Volumes : ISBN 1 84371 048 X

British Library Cataloguing-in-Publication Data
A CIP record of this title is available from the British Library

This book is printed on acid-free paper, sewn, and
cased in a durable buckram.

POLITICAL ECONOMY

FOR

THE PEOPLE.

BY

GEORGE TUCKER,

FORMERLY REPRESENTATIVE IN CONGRESS FROM VIRGINIA, AND PROFESSOR OF MORAL PHILOSOPHY IN THE UNIVERSITY OF VIRGINIA.

PHILADELPHIA:
PRINTED BY C. SHERMAN & SON.
1859.

Entered, according to Act of Congress, in the year 1859, by

GEORGE TUCKER,

in the Clerk's Office of the District Court of the United States for the Eastern District of Pennsylvania.

PREFACE.

THE following pages are, in substance, a compendium of the lectures on Political Economy delivered by the author in the University of Virginia, with such alterations and additions as his further experience and reflection have suggested.

They are now offered to the public under the belief that the subject is one of peculiar importance to a free people, whose will often directs and controls the policy of the State; and who, when they do not exert that influence, ought to know how far the sentiments of the candidates for their favor are in accordance with the true principles of national prosperity.

He has long been of opinion that there was no principle of moment in this science on which men would not, in time, be entirely agreed. Even now there are a hundred uncontroverted propositions for one which is the subject of dispute.

In his notice of those few, he has, in general, contented himself with presenting his own views, without fully stating those from which he had ventured to differ; and in subjects of no practical importance, he has not adverted to them at all. He was led to this course partly for the sake of brevity, and partly because he wished this work to have as little of a controversial character as possible.

By thus omitting the arguments which have been urged on contested questions, as well as all historical details, he flatters himself that he has set forth all the principles that are important to the national welfare.

His first object has been to state what he believed to be sound theory; and the next, to make it clear, concise, and of easy application to the affairs of social life. He dare not presume that, with all his solicitude for truth, he has always escaped error; but whenever it shall be detected, by himself or others, he will not be slow to make the correction.

PHILADELPHIA, *Oct.* 15, 1859.

CONTENTS.

CHAPTER I.

PHYSICAL CAUSES OF NATIONAL WEALTH.

CHAPTER II.

MORAL CAUSES OF NATIONAL WEALTH.

CHAPTER III.

PRINCIPLES OF VALUE.

CHAPTER IV.

PROGRESS OF SOCIETY.

CHAPTER V.

RENT.

CHAPTER VI.

DIFFERENT KINDS OF RENT.

CHAPTER VII.

LABOR.

CHAPTER VIII.

AGRICULTURAL INDUSTRY.

CHAPTER IX.

MANUFACTURING INDUSTRY.

CHAPTER X.

COMMERCIAL INDUSTRY.

CHAPTER XI.

MENTAL INDUSTRY.

CHAPTER XII.

CAPITAL.

CHAPTER XIII.

MONEY.

CHAPTER XIII.

BANKS.

CHAPTER XIV.

CONSUMPTION.

CHAPTER XVI.

PUBLIC DEBTS.

CHAPTER XVII.

THE PUBLIC EXPENDITURE.

CHAPTER XVIII.

EDUCATION.

CHAPTER XIX.

PUBLIC CHARITIES.

CHAPTER XX.

ROADS AND CANALS.

POLITICAL ECONOMY
FOR
THE PEOPLE.

CHAPTER I.

PHYSICAL CAUSES OF NATIONAL WEALTH.

WHEN we survey the nations of the earth, we perceive a great diversity among them as to refinement and civilization; and if we further consult the annals of these communities, we find that while some have gradually advanced from rudeness to refinement, as England, France, and Germany, others, which once held an elevated moral position, have descended low in the scale of civilization, as we see in Egypt, many of the nations of Asia Minor, and some of those of Ancient Greece.

The last-mentioned changes show that the condition of political communities is dependent, not wholly on physical causes, which are in the main permanent, but partly also on moral causes, or man's own efforts, which vary greatly in efficiency and degree.

The physical causes of a nation's wealth and prosperity are principally the four following: Fertility of soil, its climate, its mines, and its waters.

I. *Fertility.*—Soils differ very greatly in their power of producing articles useful to man, especially those which are fit for his subsistence—so that while some may annually return to the husbandman from twenty to a hundred times the seed he has sown, others may be utterly barren. Their fertility is mainly owing to the quantity of organic matter which they severally contain, and which once constituted portions of the living animals and vegetables they formerly supported. It also in part depends on the chemical properties of such portions of the earths and stones of which the soil is composed, and which, when reduced into small particles by the action of the elements, enter into the composition of different vegetable products.

This productive power of soils is capable of being greatly increased by human industry, partly by modes of culture, and partly by the addition of animal and vegetable manures, and of certain mineral stimulants of vegetable production, as lime, gypsum, and marl.

II. *Climate.*—The power of a country to support animal life is greatly influenced by its climate. In general, its productiveness is in proportion to the quantity of solar heat it receives, so that the nearer a country is to the Equator, the greater is its vegetable product. Of the cereal, or grain crops, while, in the Temperate Zones, there is only one in the year, there are often two in the Torrid Zone. I was once shown an acre in the Island of Antigua, which had produced eight hogsheads of sugar, equal to 8000 pounds, each pound requiring a gallon of the juice of the cane. There are also many vegetable products, highly prized by mankind, which can be produced only in warm climates. Of this description are sugar, coffee, tea, indigo, and many woods and gums. The orange, the fig, the peach, and the olive, do not thrive in high latitudes.

In the Arctic regions, the vegetable products are comparatively few and of slow growth. Fortunately, most of the *cerealia*, or grain-bearing plants, grow in the widest range of climates — from the Equator to 60° of North or South Latitude.

The heat of countries, though principally determined by their position on the globe, is also affected by two other circumstances, which it is proper to notice.

The first of these is the elevation of the region above the average level of the earth. In consequence of the perennial heat in the interior of our globe, it is found that the temperature diminishes as we ascend, at about the rate of one degree of Fahrenheit's scale for every 110 yards of ascent, so that regions of great elevation are as cold, and consequently as unfavorable to vegetable production, as lower regions much nearer to the Pole. This effect of elevation is not uniform in the different zones of the earth.

The other anomaly of climate is the difference between the eastern and western coasts of continents—it being found that the eastern are both warmer in summer, and colder in winter, than the western. This fact is the result of a local predominance of the westerly wind, and the difference of temperature on the land and the ocean, both in summer and winter. It is found that, in the Temperate Zones, there is about three times as much wind from the west as the east, in consequence of which, the prevailing west wind on the western coasts of continents has blown over the ocean, and partakes of its equable temperature, both in summer and winter—while the same excess of west wind, on the eastern coasts, has blown over land, and is consequently colder in winter and hotter in summer. Hence, the climates of Western Europe are 10° or 11° warmer in winter than on the Atlantic coast of America in the same latitude, while those on the Pacific coast are similar to those of Europe.

III. *Mines.*—The wealth and prosperity of a State are greatly affected by its minerals; the most important of which are coal, iron, copper, lead, salt, gold, and silver; each one answering its own useful purpose. England probably owes her extraordinary wealth and industry of population more to the abundance of her coal and iron than to any one single circumstance whatever. Salt seems to be indispensable to animal life, and must be brought at a great expense into countries which do not produce it.

Without the use of iron, the industry of man would be comparatively unavailing. It is, however, so extensively used, that its transportation from other countries would be very costly. The direct addition to the national wealth in the United States from their minerals, according to the census of 1840 and 1850, is only about four per cent. It will probably be doubled at the next census, principally by means of the gold of California. But this does not indicate the whole of their benefit, as, in the character of raw materials, they give a stimulus and encouragement to all the other branches of industry.

IV. *Waters.* — These, also, are very conducive to the welfare of States. Countries bounded by the ocean are able to draw from thence large supplies of wholesome and palatable food, the surplus of which they can readily exchange, by means of commerce, for such articles as their own country does not afford. Countries remote from the sea-coast may commonly obtain similar supplies from rivers and lakes.

The waters of a country also afford easy means of transportation, both of men and commodities; which is of so much importance, that hitherto there has been no large city in the world, and scarcely any second-rate one, which was not situated on the water, so that it could derive from a distance a part of its supplies by means of this cheap mode of transportation. It remains to be seen whether the new agent, steam, can furnish the like supplies with adequate cheapness.

The rivers of a country, and sometimes its lakes also, afford a cheap motive power for every species of mills, and for various kinds of manufacturing machinery.

CHAPTER II.

MORAL CAUSES OF NATIONAL WEALTH.

THESE causes are principally four—industry, skill, frugality, and good government; which we will briefly notice.

1. *Industry.*—Whatever may be the bounty of Nature, her gifts must be improved by man's own efforts, to make that bounty available; and where they are earnest and well directed, he is amply compensated for his toil. It is by means of his industry that he obtains food, clothes, houses, furniture, and utensils in countless number, to aid him in his operations on matter.

His industry is principally employed, first, in producing such raw materials as can be rendered conducive to his comfort or gratification; next, in changing the forms of those raw materials so as to make them subservient to his various purposes; and lastly, in transferring either the raw materials or the fabrics made of them from one place, where they are comparatively abundant and cheap, to another, where they are more scarce and dear. The first species of industry is chiefly agricultural, but is also, in part, that of mining and of fishing. The second is manufacturing, and the third is commercial industry.

These different species of labor are the main constituents of the material wealth of communities.

II. *Skill or knowledge.*—The exercise of man's intellectual faculties is obviously indispensable to the success of all his bodily exertions; but we mean to speak here of those powers of invention and reasoning which are above those possessed by the generality of mankind. By means of such mental superiority, man has made himself acquainted with the properties and laws of matter, and has thus rendered it subservient to his wants and purposes. In this way he has been able to find the materials of clothing at once soft, light, and warm, from the wool or hair of animals, from the fibres of certain plants, and even from the tiny web of the worm; to all of which he has imparted the most brilliant and lasting tints.

From the earth he has extracted ores, which, by a long course of patient ingenuity, he has converted into metals to assist him in his labors, and to add to the comforts and embellishments of life. From the same source, and by similar means, he has obtained glass and porcelain, stone, brick, and marble, which he has converted into houses for his comfort, churches for the worship of his Maker and Preserver, and theatres for his amusement. By his science and art, he has been enabled to traverse the boisterous and pathless ocean, and to visit the most distant regions of the globe; but more than all, he has devised a system of visible signs for the sounds of his voice, by which he can make an enduring record of his thoughts and feelings, and thus transmit to all regions, and to future generations, the useful discoveries which genius or fortunate accident may have brought to light. But the achievements of his mental powers may be best seen by looking at such results as a book, a steamship, a telescope, a microscope, a railway, a gun, or a telegraph.

In addition to those triumphs of intellect which benefit the whole human species, we often see instances of skill which are confined to particular countries and districts. In this way Sheffield is distinguished for its cutlery, Birmingham for its hardware, Manchester for its cotton fabrics, Lyons for its silks, Sèvres for its porcelain, and the Gobelin manufactory for its tapestry. So, also, Cremona once made the best violins, and Damascus and Toledo the best swords. Japan is still famous for its lacquered ware, and China for its gongs. Superior knowledge or art are thus, whether upon a small or a great scale, a source of wealth and power to their possessors.

III. *Frugality.*—If some portion of the products of industry be not put away to aid man in his future creative operations, a nation could make no progress in wealth. It could never acquire capital, which, as we shall see, is indispensable to further production. Without this aid, creative industry can no more exist than man can live without food. The extraordinary opulence of Holland, which once carried on commerce with all the world, and which even now lends money to most of its neighbors, was owing no less to the economy than the industry of its inhabitants.

One cause of wealth which has ever characterized commercial nations, is the fact that they neither could have acquired the materials of traffic, nor have extensively prosecuted it without great forbearance to spend. It is obviously as true with a nation as with an individual—if it annually consumes all that it annually produces, it at best can be but stationary, and may be easily retrograde.

IV. *Government.*—For a nation to be at once safe, prosperous, and happy, it must have the advantage of good government and laws. Man will be neither industrious nor frugal, if a rapacious government is ready to seize on the fruits of his labor. His productive powers are not likely to be much exerted, if his earnings are not secured to him, and placed beyond the reach of arbitrary power; and the spectacle of great national industry, either agricultural, manufacturing, or commercial, has never been seen under a pure despotism.

It is not only necessary that productive industry should be protected from the exactions of its own government, but also from the invasive violence of other nations. It must also be defended from the attacks of domestic force or fraud, and these defences cannot be furnished without an efficient government, and a good system of jurisprudence.

The rights of property and of person should be accurately defined, and promptly and vigorously maintained. Contracts, freely and fairly made, should be strictly enforced—and, above all, the Government should honorably fulfil its own engagements, whether they were to pay a debt, to relieve from a burden, or to concede a privilege. Nothing better shows the wise policy of honesty than a scrupulous preservation of the public faith. By a breach of it, a nation may lose more than it gains, even in a pecuniary view; but, for its loss of character, it can have no adequate compensation.

The modes in which a government may impede a nation's prosperity and wealth, are truly formidable in number and degree. It may subject its people to a merciless system of taxation, as in India, under its former Rajahs and its present rulers. It may, like Charles the Twelfth, drag them from the plough or the loom, to shed their blood to gratify his mad ambition. Or it may employ them in building vast pyramids, as in Egypt; or fantastic palaces, like the Alhambra in Spain, or Versailles in France. Or it may grant monopolies of all articles in most general use to a few pampered court favorites. Such are among the modes by which mankind have been down-trodden and oppressed by their rulers.

But governments sometimes err by a well-intended but vicious intermeddling; for in the body politic, too much regulation is as mischievous as too much medicine in the body natural. It was a conviction of this truth which suggested to the merchants of France their celebrated answer of "*laissez nous faire*"—let us alone—to Colbert, who had inquired how he could serve them. With an intelligent people, the sagacity of individuals will suggest far better schemes for their interest than any sovereign or legislature is likely to do; and, in the estimation of a free people, the forbearance of a government is one of its highest attributes.

CHAPTER III.

PRINCIPLES OF VALUE.

In laying down the following principles, I have, in most instances, conformed to the most approved theories of value; carefully avoiding, however, those subtle questions to which speculations on the subject have sometimes given rise.

1. Value, in its largest sense, is that emotion of complacency by which we regard any of our qualities or possessions that, in any way, may minister to our gratification; as health, accomplishments of body or mind, the affection or esteem of others, land, money, or goods. The most precious of these are not transferable; and while the different values set on those priceless gifts by different persons, and yet more the difference in the modes of exhibiting them, cause great diversities of moral character, they are not at all regarded by the political economist. His speculations are limited to such objects of value as can pass from individual to individual, and which thus constitute the materials of exchange.

2. The practice of exchanging commodities is so universal, and of such frequent recurrence among men, that Adam Smith has regarded it as the result

of a peculiar instinct; but it seems to require no other explanation than a reference to the predominant sway of man's self-love, in seeking to promote his interest, or add to his enjoyment, by exchanging what he values less for what he values more.

In civilized life these exchanges are indispensable not merely to man's comfort, but even to his subsistence. There, nearly all that he eats, drinks, or wears, is procured by exchanges, which it is the great use of money to facilitate; and, great as is its agency in this way, the use of credit — that is, promises, written or oral, to pay money — is far greater. If we look into the various occupations of men, we shall find that a main business of life consists either in making exchanges, or in preparing to make them. The agriculturist, by one set of exchanges, sells his raw produce, and, by another, buys comforts and luxuries for himself and his family. The manufacturer buys the raw material he requires, together with the services of his workmen, and sells the fabric he has wrought. The merchant does nothing but buy and sell. The lawyer or physician exchanges his time and skill for money, or promises to pay it. The divine, too, exchanges his efforts to make men better and wiser, for the means of supporting his household. However human efforts may be directed, they terminate in exchanging what is possessed for what is more desired.

3. In all exchanges, whether by barter (commodity

for commodity), or by sale (commodity for money), each party obtains as much, and parts with as little, as he can. Each one, however, obtains more value than he gives, but as this is the case with both parties, the articles exchanged may commonly be considered as equivalents.

4. No solitary exchange affords certain evidence of the precise value of the articles exchanged, even in the estimation of the parties, as the buyer might have given more and the seller have taken less, if necessary to the bargain. Thus, a horse is sold for one hundred dollars, but the seller might have taken ninety dollars rather than have missed the sale; and the buyer might have given an hundred and ten dollars, or more, rather than not have made the purchase. But where there is a free competition among both sellers and buyers, as is the case with articles extensively consumed, the conflicting efforts of the parties settle down on what is called the *market price.*

5. For an article to have a value that may be exchanged for another value — called, hence, its *value in exchange*, or *exchangeable value*—it must have desirableness, and be acquired with some difficulty, that is, at some cost of labor or privation. If the latter element be wanting, the article, whatever may be its utility, has no exchangeable value or price in the market. Thus air, light, and water are indispensable to men's comfort, and two of them even to his vital

existence; yet, from the abundance with which they have been furnished by nature, they generally have no exchangeable value. Let, however, the supply of these natural bounties be intercepted, and immediately their natural value gives them value in exchange. Thus, water, which in some of the West Indies is supplied wholly by rain, and is kept in cisterns or tanks, becomes, in times of long drought, an article of traffic, so that a hogshead of rum has been exchanged for a hogshead of water. Even in New York, before the Croton aqueduct, water, of a purer quality than was furnished by the neighboring springs was regularly sold. So, too, light, which, during the day, is furnished gratuitously by nature, has immense exchangeable value in the night, as is evinced by the sums expended for gas, lamps, oil, and candles. Even in the day, much is spent for the same object, in glass windows, and in lighting cellars and dark passages. Air, also, which is so abundant as to fill all space on our globe, may, under peculiar circumstances, have great exchangeable value; and there was no one of the Englishmen suffocated in the Black Hole of Calcutta, who would not have gladly given his estate for a few gallons of pure air. The same fact is manifested by the money which is occasionally expended for the ventilation required by our mansions and public edifices.

In like manner, heat, which is essential to human comfort, and which is gratuitously and profusely supplied to the inhabitants of the Torrid Zone, is purchased in the other regions of the earth at an enormous expense in fuel, warm clothing, and the construction of our buildings, public and private.

6. The difficulty of obtaining an article, which we have seen to be one of its elements of exchangeable value, is of two kinds: one consists in the labor, skill, and capital expended in its production; the other, in its relative scarcity. In the first case, the value depends upon the cost of producing it; and, supposing the labor and skill expended to be those of ordinary men, commodities will have value according to the time or labor required for their production. Thus, an article which it has cost one day to produce, will exchange for another produced in the same time. If it take as long to make a pair of shoes as a hat, supposing the materials to be of equal value, so will be the value of the hat and the shoes. Supposing it costs twice as much labor to produce a bushel of wheat as a bushel of corn, a bushel of the former will be worth two bushels of the latter.

7. In commodities, the value of which arises from the scarcity, that value is determined by the offers of rival competitors. Of this character are those articles which cannot, like those of the first class, be indefinitely multiplied, or, perchance, be increased at all, as paintings by old masters, antique sculptures, coins, medals, or manuscripts; and so, of any other rare product of art or nature.

8. Of such articles, the owner has the monopoly, or sole right of sale, which is more or less exclusive, according to the scarcity. Monopolies of articles liberally consumed, and susceptible of an abundant production, are sometimes granted by arbitrary governments, and sometimes they may be, in any country, the result of fortunate accident. The exclusive rights which are, for a time, conferred on authors and inventors, are monopolies created by law. In all these cases, the monopolist having the power of fixing his own price, and knowing that the extent of his sales will be inversely as the price, will choose between the alternatives of selling a less quantity at a high price, or a large quantity at a low price. The demand he has no means of influencing except by the price.

9. In both classes of commodities, whatever may be the price at any one time or place, that price is liable to fluctuation by reason of an alteration in the supply or the demand, that is to say, in the relation between them; for if the same alterations take place both in the supply and the demand, whether by increase or diminution, then the price will not be affeoted.

10. By the *supply* of a commodity is meant, not the whole quantity of it in the community, but only that portion which is offered for sale in the market, or ready to be so offered: such are the shoes in the shops of the shoemakers and others; the hats and other fabrics in the appropriate places of sale; the

provisions of different kinds in the stores of their respective dealers.

11. By the *demand* of a commodity is meant the desire to possess it, combined with the means of purchasing it, to which may be added the will to use the means. The desire of a poor man for a costly luxury has no influence on its price, and the desire of a rich miser may be as unavailing as that of a beggar.

12. Every addition to the supply—the demand continuing the same—tends to lower the price, since it is only by a reduction of price that the additional quantity can be generally sold. A diminished demand, producing the same relative change as an increased supply, has the same lowering effect.

13. A diminished supply, on the other hand, or an increased demand, tends to raise the price, since it is only by giving a higher price that the quantity desired can be certainly obtained. The rise of price is sometimes the effect of competition among the buyers, and sometimes the result of the sagacity of the sellers, who raise the price in anticipation of the increased competition of the buyers.

14. It must not, however, be supposed, as sometimes has been done, that a change in the supply or demand of an article produces a proportional change of price. The alteration of the price is always in a less ratio than that of the supply or demand. Thus, let it be assumed that the supply of a commodity has been doubled, the demand being unchanged—the

natural consequence of this addition to the supply is a fall of price; but the consequence as natural and certain of such fall of price is an increased demand for the commodity, which, we have seen, tends to raise the price; so that before the price has fallen to one-half, which would be in proportion to the double supply, the demand and supply are equal, and the price is, of course, stationary. In this way the addition to the supply is met partly by a reduction of price, and partly by an increased demand. Hence, the great increase of gold and silver, consequent on the discovery of America, and which was estimated at ten times their previous amount, did not reduce the value of those metals to one-tenth, but only to one-third or one-fourth — the additional supply being counterbalanced partly by the fall of price, and partly by the increased demand* for those metals, in consequence of their reduced value.

15. In like manner, a diminished supply, by raising the price, lessens the demand, and to that extent

---

* M. Say, whose views on political economy are commonly clear as well as just, has fallen into a singular error on this subject. He estimates the increased demand of the precious metals at *twenty-five* times the amount before the discovery of America. Had this been the case, the value of those metals must have been raised instead of lowered by the product of the American mines. Had the demand been only *ten* times as great — equal to the increase of the supply—the value would have been unchanged. It gives almost as much surprise that so palpable an error should have been unnoticed, both by the English translator and the American editor of Say.

prevents a rise of price equivalent to the diminution of the supply.

16. It thus appears that every alteration, either in the demand or the supply of a commodity, produces not only a change of price, but that, by reason of this change of price, an increase or diminution of the one produces, in a less degree, a correspondent increase or diminution of the other.

17. There is, in every community, a precise and certain demand for every commodity, — comprehending its different kinds, — according to the desirableness of each article, and the difficulty of obtaining it; which difficulty is chiefly its price. Thus, in the case of hats, we will suppose, by way of illustration, the demand for that article of apparel to be as follows, according to the price:

For hats	whose price was	five dollars,	the demand	to be	1000.
"	"	four dollars,	"	"	2000.
"	"	three dollars,	"	"	6000.
"	"	two dollars,	"	"	10,000.
"	"	one dollar,	"	"	20,000.

18. This may be called the natural demand, founded on the existing tastes and means of the community; and to this demand the makers of hats must conform, or incur a loss; for if they make the supply exceed this natural demand, as if they were to make 2000 hats whose cost of production or natural price was five dollars, the natural demand for which was only 1000, they could not sell the extra

thousand without a reduction of price. If, on the other hand, they made but 500 hats of that quality, although for them they might obtain a higher price, the profits thus obtained would be less than would be afforded by the sale of a thousand hats at five dollars, according to the laws of value previously stated.

19. Value, being a feeling of the mind, is as various as the diversified and ever-changing wants and tastes of men. It is different in different objects, in the same object at different times and places, with different individuals, and with the same individual, on different occasions. On a dreary journey, a draught of water may be more valuable than a gallon of wine.

20. As value can be known only by its manifestations in acts of exchange, its different degrees must be estimated by comparing the values thus exchanged; but as all of such values are liable to alteration, there cannot be that uniform measure of value which is afforded to portions of matter, space, or time. Although, therefore, such a precise and unvarying standard is unattainable, certain objects, which, under particular circumstances, make the nearest approaches to uniformity, have been selected as qualified measures of value.

21. Of these measures, one is best for one purpose and another for another. The precious metals, so highly and so universally prized, and otherwise strongly recommended, afford the best measure for

the same time and place. For most objects of exchangeable value, they then and there furnish, for all practical purposes, an exact measure. Thus, if an ounce of silver exchange in the market for a bushel of wheat, weighing sixty pounds, and also for two bushels of maize, or for ten pounds of beef, it follows that one bushel of wheat is equal in value to two bushels of maize, and one pound of beef to six pounds of wheat. But these metals vary greatly in value in different countries, according to their respective distances from the most productive mines of the world. They are thus more valuable in Asia than in Europe, and in Europe than America. Their value has varied yet more in different ages of the world.

22. Labor, which regulates the value of so many articles useful to man, has also been deemed a fit measure of value in different countries, from the similarity of mankind in their ruling propensities and desires, and their obedience to the laws of their common nature; yet we find that human labor is far more willing and efficient in the Temperate than in either the Torrid or the Frigid Zones. Its value varies, too, from moral causes.

23. Corn, some species of which constitute a chief article of subsistence to civilized man, and which is so readily converted into human labor, has also been regarded as a fit measure of value. It has, however, no more uniformity than labor; and, from the diver-

sity of human aliment, has a less extensive application. Besides, it has been found that, in the progressive increase of population, corn gradually increases in value, from its greater difficulty of attainment; and that labor gradually falls in value, from its greater abundance, as will be hereafter more fully explained.

24. On this account, a combination of corn and labor has been suggested as affording the best measure for comparing values at different periods, and between countries in different stages of advancement. The plan is plausible in theory, but it has as yet furnished no rules of practical application.

25. But notwithstanding these inherent disadvantages, human reason has, by numerous comparisons, been able to deduce the values of objects, at any time or place, in their countless diversity, with an approximation to the truth which is sufficient for any purpose of practical utility, or the gratification of a liberal curiosity.

CHAPTER IV.

THE PROGRESS OF SOCIETY.

SUCH are the principles of exchangeable value which we perceive have their foundation in the innate desires and propensities of man. Let us now see their application to the three great sources of national wealth: the RENT OF LAND, the WAGES OF LABOR, and the PROFITS OF CAPITAL — and first of RENT.

In the infancy of society, when population was thin, land, however productive, was, from its abundance, like air, light, or water, without exchangeable value, and was the common property of the little tribe or community which chanced to occupy it. In the progressive increase of population, according to the great law of all animated nature, it ultimately became private property, and, from its increased difficulty of attainment, together with its utility, it acquired exchangeable value, which gradually augmented until it yielded a rich return in rent. The sources and modes of this gradual advancement in value will be better understood by attending to the progress of society in its different stages of civilization.

In the first of these stages, according both to

present observation and the annals of history, men lived in very small communities, which were banded together more by the social instinct than by the force of government or of laws; and their sustenance was derived from the wild game of the forest, or its spontaneous fruits, such as we now see in the North American Indians, in the savage inhabitants of Southern Africa, of Australia, or of New Zealand; and such were the primitive inhabitants of Gaul, Britain, and other portions of the old world. Though each of these communities may have had its peculiarities, by reason of a diversity of physical circumstances, or from accidental circumstances, the aborigines of this continent, in their principal features, may be considered the type of all the rest.

The sole occupations of the Indian are hunting and war, which he pursues at intervals with indefatigable ardor; but, when not so excited, he passes his time in smoking, or in listless inactivity. His mental powers, concentrated on few objects, are little developed, but the qualities of his heart are in full vigor. Sometimes warm in his attachments, but still more implacable in his resentments, he is occasionally generous, but always vindictive and cruel. He discharges the rites of hospitality with scrupulous exactness, according to his notions, and he may even instal his guest into the place of the relative he has lost. He commonly shows a high sense of justice in his little dealings, but yet more by enforcing the laws of retaliation against others, and even by submitting himself in turn to its hardest decrees. He exhibits great courage in braving danger, and yet more in enduring pain when subjected to torture by his enemies; but when tempted by pleasure, he is incapable of self-command. He is thus by turns a hero, a sot, a glutton, and sometimes a polygamist. To his children he is over-indulgent; is respectful to age; but the women he treats as drudges and slaves, to which treatment, however, they submit rather with pride than a sense of degradation.

Though, in this stage of society, no individual had an exclusive right to any portion of the soil, except during his temporary occupation of it, yet the whole community claimed property in the large district which constituted their hunting-ground, and which had its boundaries assigned by rivers, mountains, and other physical marks. These claims were firmly maintained, and constituted the most frequent cause of war with neighboring tribes. They have always been recognized by the United States, and have been the foundation of many a treaty of cession by the Indians for large pecuniary considerations.

In this, the hunter state, the means of subsistence being wholly or principally dependent on the chase, are very precarious; and there are probably more instances of extreme suffering from the want of food among the sequestered tribes of Indians than are to be found in the densest districts of China. From the precariousness of subsistence among these tribes, together with the exterminating character of their wars, population increases slowly with them, and, occasionally, not at all. The same circumstances, but for the approach of the white race, might have postponed, to an indefinite period, the transition of the Indian race to a higher stage of social existence. The density of population of hunter tribes is commonly rated at one person to the square mile, or 640 acres; but that of the Indians within the United States has been more nearly one to 1000 acres.

Tribes, in this stage of civilization, living on the coast, or prolific lakes and rivers, sometimes derive their principal subsistence from fish. Such tribes have nearly the same characteristics as those who live by hunting, except, perhaps, that their supplies of food are less precarious. Here began the noble art of navigation, by which the rude canoe has, after a thousand improvements, grown to the floating fortress of one hundred guns, the magnificent merchant ship, and lastly, the steamer which flies over the water like a bird through the air.

The *Pastoral* state is generally regarded as the second stage of civilization. It probably originated in this way: when the population of a hunter tribe had continued to increase, notwithstanding its inherent obstacles, and it pressed more heavily on the means of subsistence, the sagacity of some individual, or other fortunate accident, first showed the practicability of taming and domesticating some of the wild animals of the forest, by which man would provide for himself a farther supply of food. The first instance would soon be followed by others, until the practice of breeding and rearing animals whose flesh, or milk, or skins afforded him sustenance or raiment, became the general occupation of all. In this way, the means of subsistence ceased to be precarious, and could support ten, or perhaps twenty times as many as the same district could support by hunting.

By some such process, man won from their original wildness the cow, the sheep, the goat, the hog; and of birds, that most useful species which supplies us with eggs and chickens, and which, from its excellence, is called "the fowl," ducks, and geese, to which America has added the turkey, furnishing man with food equally palatable and nourishing; and, to serve other useful purposes, the camel, the horse, the elephant, and the dog, which prefers the society of man to that of his own species, and which remains faithful to him when deserted by all other friends.

But every country is not adapted to the pastoral state. Some regions are not naturally productive of grass, or not in sufficient quantity; and man, in his social progress, must pass from the hunter state to the agricultural. Such must have been the destiny of the aborigines of North America, which is everywhere, except in the prairies of the West, covered with a dense forest. The Indians had accordingly made more advances towards the agricultural than the pastoral state, as they had succeeded in taming no bird or beast, but had their little patches of tobacco, maize, and cymlings.*

The nations and tribes of Western Asia, spoken of in the five books of Moses, were essentially pastoral. Abraham is mentioned as rich in "cattle, silver, and in gold;" and Lot, his rival in wealth and power, has "flocks, and herds, and tents;" and when the Egyptians were suffering from a drought, Joseph gave them bread in exchange for "horses, and for the flocks, and for the cattle of the herds, and for the asses." So, when the laws against the invasion of property are stated, "oxen, asses, and sheep" hold a conspicuous place.

In the pastoral state, the character of the population undergoes a great change. From being warlike it has become pacific, though not unfit for war in defence of its rights, and sometimes even for conquest. With manners more humane and civilized, the mental powers are also farther developed by more frequent and varied exercise. Men now had leisure for the simpler manufactures, for which they had new materials and new incentives; and here, without doubt, wool was first spun and woven. Exchanges, which had been rare in the hunter state,

* The "squashes" of the Northern States.

where everything is consumed as soon as produced, naturally increased with the means. By the greater facility and more abundant supply of subsistence thus afforded, population gradually grew to ten or twenty times what it had been in the hunter state.

But, soon or late, the members of a community would reach the level first of easy, then of difficult subsistence; when the increased demand for food would stimulate to new efforts for a further supply, which could be furnished only by agriculture. The land, indeed, had always made some small direct contribution of human aliment, but the quantity could be greatly multiplied, partly by breaking up and loosening the soil, and partly by ridding it of all noxious or useless plants, and limiting its products exclusively to those articles which afford sustenance to man.

Before the introduction of the useful arts, and especially that of making iron for axes, spades, ploughs, and other tools, the progress of agriculture would be slow. Without those efficient aids, the earth could be rid of its trees and shrubs only by the imperfect process of fire, and be turned up by still inferior substitutes for iron. But after a community had, by means of its own invention, or the exchanges of commerce, acquired the use of this metal, population would obtain a new spring, and be gradually so augmented, that the square mile which had once afforded precarious subsistence to a single savage might, under favorable circumstances, afford an easier and better one to two or three hundred, or even more; for the highest degree of density of numbers which the soil can support has never yet been reached. The growing value of land, and of its annual returns, in this third and last stage of society, we will now proceed to consider.

CHAPTER V.

RENT.

LAND, which had probably become private property in the pastoral state, would certainly become so in the agricultural state. As every material thing, useful to man, is directly or indirectly derived from the soil, it always possessed the first element of exchangeable value, and, as soon as, by the progress of population, it had relative scarcity, or even in anticipation of it, it would also have the second element, and be appropriated by those who chanced to possess power or influence. When once its ownership in perpetuity had a value in exchange or price, so also must its ownership for a year, when its most valuable products are regularly renewed. This is the origin of RENT, which is the necessary consequence of the utility and relative scarcity of land.

In amount, the rent of land is the excess of its products beyond the labor and capital expended in its cultivation, according to the existing rates of remuneration. Such will be the clear profit of the proprietor, if he himself be the cultivator; or, supposing such excess to accord with the average product, in good and bad seasons, it would be the measure of the rent which a tenant could afford to pay, and the landlord be willing to receive. Thus, suppose the average annual product of a piece of land to be 100 bushels of wheat, and that 70 bushels would remunerate the labor and capital spent in its culture, then 30 bushels, the residue, would be the clear annual profit or rent.

When land is abundant, compared with the population, the price of labor, from its relative scarcity, will, according to the laws of value, be naturally high, and that of land and its products, from their abundance, will be low. Rents, therefore, which are the excess in value of those products above the cost of cultivation, will also be low. But as, from the continual increase of population, there is a growing demand for raw produce, and the supply cannot, from the limited extent and productiveness of the soil, be proportionally augmented, there will be a gradual rise in the price of raw produce, and consequently of rents. This rise is as natural and certain as is the rise of corn after a bad harvest. There is, in both cases, the same relative alteration between the supply and demand—the only difference being that, in case of a short harvest, the effect is produced by a deficient supply, but in the other (that of a growing population) it is produced by an increased demand.*

Such would be the rise and progress of rents, if all

---

* The same process may be effected by the co-operation of poor laborers, as we see in the familiar practice of *log-rolling*.

the land was fertile, uniform in quality, and nearly equi-distant from market, as are the Delta of Egypt, the American bottom in the State of Illinois, and a few other favored spots on the globe; for a difference of fertility, or distance from market, has no more agency in *originating* rent, than has a difference of color. But in point of fact, there is, in almost every country of tolerable extent, a gradation of soils, varying from great fertility to utter barrenness, which, after the increased demands of a growing population have given existence to rent, do make that rent higher or lower, according to their respective degrees of fertility.

In this diversity of soils, the lands first cultivated are those which are at once most fertile, most accessible, and most easily cultivated. Some of the richest are, in a state of nature, most heavily timbered, and it devolves on those who have the greatest command of capital and labor* to clear lands of this description—it being a matter of calculation, whether it be more profitable to cultivate the richest land, at a greater expense, or inferior lands at a less. But in no long time, the rich alluvial lands are certain to be taken into cultivation.

As population advances, and the demand for raw produce consequently increases, soils of less fertility, yielding less clear profit, will naturally be taken into cultivation to furnish the required supply, which

* Chapter I., §§ 12, 13.

must be obtained at a greater cost of labor. But, to attribute the rise of raw produce which then exists, to this resort to poorer soils, is to mistake an effect for a cause. Raw produce does not rise because inferior soils, yielding a less return to the labor and capital expended on them, are resorted to, but such soils are cultivated in consequence of the rise of raw produce, caused by the increase of population. If raw produce had not previously risen, the inferior soils could not have been taken into cultivation without the prospect of loss.

It is obvious, from what has been said, that land must have a degree of fertility more than sufficient to defray the cost of cultivation, before it can yield a rent; yet this limit is constantly receding from the lands of the best quality, and extending the field of cultivable land as the price of raw produce rises.

But while land may be too poor to remunerate the cost of cultivating it, it can rarely ever fail, in a peopled country, to yield some annual profit, and, consequently, rent. It spontaneously furnishes fuel for warmth and cooking, the means of shelter from the elements, different kinds of wild animals and birds, which will more than repay the labor of taking them, as well as pasturage for cattle.

There are several circumstances which check and retard, without arresting the gradual rise of raw produce, by augmenting its supply:

First. The resort to poorer and poorer soils, the

cultivation of which is made profitable only by the previous rise of raw produce, and which thus aids in meeting the increasing demand for food.

Secondly. By drawing supplies from a greater distance. The extent of this resource depends upon the facilities of transportation. In a country of which roads are bad, this source of supply has a narrow field of action; but when there are good roads and canals, supplies can be obtained from a distance proportioned to the saving in the cost of carriage. Since the introduction of iron railways, supplies may now be obtained from a distance perhaps of one hundred miles at as small a cost as was formerly required for their transportation in a wagon twenty-five or thirty miles.

Thirdly. Increasing the productiveness of the soil by an outlay of capital in the purchase of manures and vegetable stimulants, such as guano, gypsum, and the like. These often increase the value of the products of the soil far beyond their cost; and it sometimes may be so great as to make the increased supply exceed the increased demand, and thus, for the time, lower the price of raw produce. But even then, inasmuch as the landlord gains more by the increased quantity than he loses by the fall of price, rents would thereby be raised.* To the above tem-

---

* It deserves to be remarked that all these three expedients for increasing the supplies of raw produce to meet the demand of growing numbers have been referred to for the purpose of

porary checks to the advance in price of raw produce we may add improvements in husbandry; whether by the mode of tillage, the rotation of crops, or by ameliorating processes, such as the turnip or clover culture. But these improvements, like the use of manures, while they tend to lower the price of raw produce by augmenting the supply beyond the temporary demand, tend also to raise rents:

First. Because, whatever may be the addition to the supply of the means of subsistence, population will ultimately raise the demand to the same level; and, the price being also thereby raised, rents must continue to rise.

Secondly. Without waiting for a further increase of mouths to be fed, the immediate effect of such improvements is to raise rents; since here, as in the increased supply of raw produce, from a further outlay of capital, as already mentioned, the landlord will gain more by the addition to the quantity than he would lose by the reduction of price.

It has indeed been maintained by writers of reputation that the effect of improvements in agriculture, whether in saving labor or increasing the productiveness of the soil, is to lower rents; but this conclusion seems to be directly at variance with the laws of

---

explaining the rise and progress of rent, though they, — the two first always, and the third partially, — as well as rent, are the natural effect of the rise of raw produce, caused by the increase of population.

value and price. The natural effect of such improvements is unquestionably to lessen the price of raw produce; but an increased demand and consumption would then be as natural a consequence as had been the fall of price; and such increased demand, checking the fall of price before the reduction was in proportion to the enlarged supply, the market value of the whole crop would be greater than it had previously been; and the clear profit or rent would consequently be higher.

The preceding view cannot be impugned except by assuming that the demand for raw produce, in proportion to the population, is a fixed quantity, which cannot be increased. But the great difference in the corn crops of every country, according to the seasons,—they being twice or thrice as much in a good season as a bad one,—shows that the consumption even of corn is susceptible of great contraction or expansion, according to the greater or less abundance of the supply. When the supply is small, the consumption is lessened, partly from choice, but still more from necessity; and cheaper food is substituted for the more costly. But when the supply is large, the consumption is more liberal, both as to the quantity and quality; and there is more waste, more dispensed in charity, more consumed in manufactures, and lastly, more, from the reduced price, can find a market at a distance. If these were not the natural consequences of an increased production, the agricultural class would gain more by a short crop — supposing it to be general — than by a large one; and the instinctive sagacity of self-interest would be at fault with farmers when they pray, as they ever do, for fruitful seasons, though their neighbors should share in the same good fortune, and when they feel assured that in bad seasons no rise of price can adequately compensate them for the shortness of the crops. Another circumstance which tends to raise rents is the improvement in the means of transportation by canals and roads. The chief cause of the difference between the prices of raw produce in two places is the cost of transportation; and all, or nearly all, that can be saved of this expense, is so much added to the exchangeable value of the produce.

The same saving also enlarges the sphere of the market, and causes a traffic between places, which, at the previous cost of transport, could not be carried on without loss. Thus, by means of railways, the oyster trade is now extended from the Atlantic coast to every portion of the interior; and though many places may, in this way, lose a portion of their former supplies of provisions, yet this loss may be compensated, or more than compensated, by the new supplies then afforded from more distant districts. Thus, if New York now draw off from Philadelphia much of the butter, milk, poultry, and fruits, with which the latter city had been previously supplied, she, in turn, is also furnished with new supplies of the like articles from more distant sources, by which enlarged traffic, both buyers and sellers, that is, both producers and consumers, are benefited.

In truth, a very considerable portion of the labor of every community is expended, not in the business of producing or fabricating commodities, but merely in transporting these products of industry from one place to another, where they have greater value; and whatever can be saved of this expense of transport is so much added to the revenue of the community.

There are circumstances which have a direct tendency to lower rents. One of these is a diminution of the population, however caused, whether by epidemic diseases, scarcity, or emigration — always supposing that the population was not previously too dense for the whole of it to be profitably employed. This redundancy of numbers seemed to have existed in Ireland a few years since; for, after an efflux of population so great as to make the numbers less by the census of 1851 than they had been by the census of 1841, an encouragement was given to the employment of labor which benefited the community as well as the laboring classes, and consequently raised rents.

The emigration which is continually taking place from the Southern to the Western and Southwestern

States, tends to keep rents stationary in the first-named States; and, in some few districts which have declined in population, rents may have somewhat diminished.

Taxation is another cause of the fall of rents. A tax on the land being so much taken from its profits, is the same as so much taken from rent. A tax on labor, too, by increasing the cost of cultivation, would have a similar tendency.

Town lots, like land in the country, have a price, and consequently yield a rent according to the profit which they can afford to the occupant. But the sources of profit in the two cases are very different. In the case of arable land, the profit arises from the productiveness of the soil, but in the case of town lots it arises from the facilities afforded to industry.

Men are induced to congregate in cities and towns, partly by the social instinct, and partly for the benefits of co-operation, by which many things are done sooner and better than could be effected by a single individual, and many more which he could not perform at all.

The proportion of the population thus congregated is apt to increase with the increasing density of numbers. In the United States, where the population is as yet thin, the cities and towns of above three thousand inhabitants, contained but one-sixth of the whole population in 1850. In 1840, they contained not one-tenth. In England, such towns contain about one-half of the population.

They are more favorable to the cultivation of science and the arts of every kind. If they also more favor human depravity and misery, they afford readier means of punishing the one, and of alleviating the other. The modes of human happiness are so different in town and country life, that it is difficult to compare them; but whatever may be the result of the comparison, the constant tendency of cities, in all free and industrious communities, to increase, is inevitable.

Cities and towns, according to the numbers there congregated, offer the best field for buying and selling, and obtaining the profits of commerce. Lots, therefore, increase in value with the size of the town, until a certain point is reached, and the rents of such lots will be in proportion to their price. As a general rule, a site for a shop in a city is valuable in proportion to the number of persons who have a ready access to it, which number will be partly in proportion to the population of the city, and partly to the accessibility of the particular site — twenty, or even fifty, times as many persons commonly passing in a day by one lot or site, as in some others. The same circumstances which raise the value of the lots, in the same degree raise the rents, so that while lots generally in small towns, and some of them on the borders of large ones, may sell for little more than land in the vicinity, others may sell for a hundred times as much.

Other circumstances may occasionally enhance the value of town lots, as when they afford pleasant prospects, are open to pure air, or are in agreeable neighborhoods; but it is the advantage which some sites possess over others for traffic which constitutes their highest pecuniary value. In the same degree that cities thrive in business, and increase in population, the shops improve in the extent, the variety, and the attractiveness of their wares, and rents rise in proportion. When the population diminishes, rents proportionally decline.

The rent paid for houses in town consists, in addition to the rent of the lot, of the interest on the cost of the building, with some allowance for ordinary repairs, and gradual decay.

It may be remarked that land, including lots and houses in town, yield less than the average profits of capital, partly on account of the greater security of the capital, and partly because, being visible to all, and appreciable by all, they confer on the proprietor somewhat more of influence in society than personal property.

It often happens, in cities, that one person owns the house, and another the ground on which it stands. For this, the owner of the house pays a ground-rent, and the house is a security for its payment. It is thus a favorite mode of investment with capitalists, and hence nearly all the houses in London pay a ground-rent. It, however, occasionally happens in declining towns, or when buildings have been erected on sites unfavorable to business, or beyond its demands, that the house and lot together will not sell for as much as will pay the ground-rent.

CHAPTER VI.

THE DIFFERENT SPECIES OF RENT.

It often happens that the proprietor of land wants the skill, or the capital, or the inclination to cultivate it, and by renting it, he, the tenant, and the State would be gainers. The benefit may, however, be materially affected by the length of the term for which the land is rented. In long leases, the tenant is interested in manuring the soil, and in making other improvements; but in short ones, his interest is rather a present than a future profit, and to expend no money which will not give an immediate or a short return.

In the United States, where, from the cheapness of land, so many are able to buy it, and where almost every man hopes to own it, leases from year to year, to be terminated at the pleasure of either party, after notice, are very common; and the landlord endeavors to guard against their inherent disadvantages by strict stipulations as to the course of cultivation, the rotation of crops, manuring, and the like; but these engagements, being often evaded, or unfaithfully executed, are prolific of dispute and mutual discontent. Probably England owes the excellence of her husbandry to no one thing so much as long leases.

Lands are sometimes rented for a proportional part of the crop; which proportion varies from a fourth to a half, according to the richness of the soil; and occasionally for more than a half, as in the case of meadows, and spots of extraordinary fertility. The difference of profit between the best and the worst arable soils is yet greater than the difference of rent stated; but as, in this country, there is little land rented which has not its value to the tenant enhanced by a dwelling-house, fences, and other improvements, there are scarcely any portions, however poor, which rent for less than one-fourth. Even as to these inferior soils, there is, in the first settled States, more competition among the class of renters than that of landlords. The proportion for rent is greatest in the most densely peopled States.

Very frequently land is rented for an annual sum of money which is somewhat less than its estimated value; the proprietor preferring the certainty of a smaller sum to the mere chance of a larger one. This is the general mode of renting in England. It is the best method in a rich country.

There is another kind of rent, where the land is cultivated at the joint expense of the landlord and tenant, who divide the produce between them. This is called the *Metayer* system. It prevails extensively in France and other parts of continental Europe, and is not unfrequent in the United States. It admits of infinite modifications, as to the proportion which the parties respectively provide of the live stock, the seed, taxes, and implements of husbandry. Here, too, the terms of the bargain are most advantageous to the landlord in the most densely populated districts.

The metayer system has been generally condemned by English writers, as liable to the objections made to short leases, and as favoring improvident culture. Yet some parts of Europe where it prevails have a prosperous and happy tenantry.

In the northern half of the United States, the larger proprietors of the land cultivate it by hired laborers; in which case, the rent or profits of the soil are combined with the profits of capital.

In the southern division, the larger tracts of land are generally cultivated by slaves, while many of the small tracts are tilled by their proprietors. In both cases, the profits of the land are combined with those both of labor and capital.

In all cases in which land is cultivated by the proprietor, a considerable part of the profits of the soil consists in the supplies furnished to his family in fuel, and in various kinds of aliment, as meats, poultry, milk, butter, and garden stuff, which commonly amount to a respectable rent, though they are often overlooked in the estimates made of the profits of landed property.

Rent of Mines.—Various minerals useful to man are also sources of rent. They differ from arable land in this important particular: they possess not, like the fertility of the soil, the advantage of being perpetually renewed by the spontaneous bounty of nature; but they have been stored away, by the same benignant agency, in the bowels of the earth, whence they are drawn at great cost, and always by a diminution of their quantity. It depends upon the cost of working them, and their relative scarcity, whether they are able to yield rent; for when these minerals are very abundant near the surface of the earth, their price may not be more than sufficient to repay the labor and capital expended in bringing them to market.

One of the most valuable of these minerals is coal, as fuel, both for household purposes and for manufactures, especially for the fabrication of iron. It is to this mineral that England is mainly indebted for the great extent and excellence of her manufactures; for it constitutes the fuel of her steam-engines, which furnish her, at a moderate cost, with an unlimited motive power.

As population increases, the demand for coal has a correspondent increase, but the cost of extracting it from its native beds naturally augments as the mines grow deeper. This additional cost may, however, be counterbalanced by improved machinery and a larger application of capital. Should the increased demand for coal have more effect in raising its price than the counteractions mentioned have in lowering it, then all of its increased value, beyond the cost of bringing it to market, would be rent. In this way, coal-mines, exempt from neighboring competition, sometimes yield a high rent.

Next to coal, iron is the mineral most extensively used by man. It has, however, been furnished in such abundance by nature, that its ordinary price merely repays the labor and capital expended in converting its ore into metal, with a more or less liberal profit, without yielding any rent. Furnaces and forges for making iron may indeed be occasionally leased, but the consideration paid by the tenant, which is called a rent, like that paid for houses, is merely an interest on the capital expended on the buildings and machinery. Where, however, the machinery of these establishments is worked by running water, the gift of nature, this moving-power, like that of mills, may be an exception, and yield an annual rent.

Mines of the precious metals, when they can be monopolized, may yield a large rent, as the value of the products may greatly exceed the cost of obtaining them. Where the lands containing the precious metals are free to be worked by all, and when the yield is so great as it has been in California and Australia, the profits being the joint result of the bounty of nature and the industry of man, seem in part analogous to rent; and where spots of extraordinary richness are regarded by custom as the property of the occupants, they may be sold and transferred to others—in which case, the compensation received has all the features of rent.

The time may come when all the auriferous lands in California and Australia will be private property, and yield, according to their richness, an annual profit to the proprietor, whether he work them himself, or let them to a tenant.

Salt-mines and springs occasionally afford a rent. This mineral, so useful as a condiment to our food, and for preserving meat and fish from putrefaction, as well as for its extensive use in the laboratory and in manufactures, has been furnished by nature in such profusion, that its quantity, principally in a state of solution, would be sufficient, if separated from the water, to cover the whole surface of our globe with a layer of salt probably more than a hundred feet deep. But with all this abundance, there are many districts of country which obtain this commodity from a great distance. In the United States, the Atlantic portion is supplied principally from Liverpool and Turks Island. The Western States are supplied from the salt-works of New York, Virginia, and Pennsylvania.

When salt springs or mines are solitary, or nearly so, they may yield a very high rent. The proprietor, having a monopoly of this indispensable article, is able to obtain a liberal price for a large quantity in the sale of which he has no competitor. This was the case with Preston's salt-works on the Holstein, in Virginia. He found a vent for all that he made at a dollar a bushel; but an enterprising rival having purchased a piece of land in the vicinity, on which, as he rightly conjectured, salt water from the same spring could be found, sunk a well, and at a great depth obtained water still more strongly impregnated with salt than Preston's. To secure the monopoly entirely to himself, he then rented Preston's spring for $10,000 a year, and closed it up. In this way the public was deprived of the effect of competition, and of the full benefit of the bounty of nature.

On the Kanawha, in the same State, salt springs are found to an extent of several miles on the banks of the river, and there salt is produced to the amount of many millions of bushels in a year. The salt works at Salina, in the interior of New York, are still more productive. Such of these springs as have extraordinary richness, are rented according to the average value of their annual product beyond the cost of making the salt.

In time of war, salt is here extensively manufactured from sea water, and, to some extent, in time of peace. Should the springs which now furnish so large a part of the quantity consumed, become in process of time exhausted, or too weak to repay the cost of working them, the water of the ocean may become our only domestic resource.

Fisheries are also a source of rent. The shores of the Potomac, and some other of our principal rivers, abound in the spring with shad and herring, but there are particular spots on their banks which are alone adapted to hauling the seine — the only way in which those fish can be taken in large quantities. Sometimes the proprietor of a fishery prefers renting it to retaining it for his own use; and, since sometimes as many as 100,000 fish are taken at a single draught, these fisheries are very profitable, and their rent is proportionally high.

Wharves, quays, and the like facilities to commerce, are frequent subjects of rent.

In all these cases of mines, salt-works, fisheries, mills, and other productive establishments, as in the instance of cultivated land, whenever, from the relation between the supply and the demand, the value of the commodity produced exceeds the cost of producing it, such excess is rent, which is received either wholly by the proprietor, or partly by him and partly by his tenant, the temporary occupant.

CHAPTER VII.

ON LABOR.

It would be to little purpose that man had been liberally furnished with valuable materials, if they were not also improved, by his industry and skill, into the means of ministering to his wants and comforts. Behold the untutored savage, earning with great effort a subsistence from the wild game of the forest, which is, moreover, so precarious that he sometimes perishes from want, spending his life, when not engaged in hunting or war, in a torpor both of body and mind. Compare him now with the civilized man, surrounded by the benefits of a well-ordered household, adding to the gratifications of his physical nature the pleasures of reading, of music, of conversation, and the numberless enjoyments of civilized life. All these advantages he owes to the exertions of his own industry and skill, and to the industry and skill of those who had preceded him, or who now co-operate with him.

He has rendered the mineral, the animal, and the vegetable world subservient to his various purposes. One species of mineral earth, he, by dint of great labor, converts into iron, which is again transformed into tools and instruments of various forms and dimensions, from an anchor or steam-engine to the balance-spring of a watch, or a cambric needle. He uses gold and silver for one set of purposes, and the baser metals of copper, tin, lead, and zinc for others. He multiplies the utility of the precious metals by converting them into leaves of extreme thinness, and has coined them into money, by which he saves himself infinite labor in exchanging that which he can spare for that which he wants. He draws from the bowels of the earth fuel to keep him warm, and to support the fires required by the operations of his ingenuity and art; salt, also, to preserve his meat, and render his food at once palatable and wholesome; and numerous other minerals, useful as medicines or for manufactures.

From the animal world he derives materials both for his food and his clothing. From one portion he obtains furs, from another wool, which, by a long train of ingenious processes, he converts into clothing at once soft, light, and warm. From a worm his indefatigable industry has obtained the materials of a yet more brilliant and ornamental apparel; and to all these he imparts dyes that rival the hues of the rainbow. The skins of some animals he converts into leather, of different descriptions, and adapted to various uses; and from the bristles of the hog, the filthiest of all animals, he fabricates twenty kinds of brushes to serve the purposes of cleanliness in his person and dwelling. The largest terrestrial animal furnishes him with ivory for one set of uses, and the largest marine animal with whalebone for another set. He uses the camel and the horse, as well as the elephant, for transportation, and to assist his operations both in peace and war. The dog is his willing slave, to aid him in killing other animals that are either noxious or serve for food. He does not confine his powers to the land; he descends to the rivers and sea, and drains from them in unexhaustible abundance food equally palatable and nutritious.

He has, by the art of navigation, gradually improved by numberless ingenious inventions, encountered and overcome the dangers of the ocean, has visited regions placed at the farthest extremities of the earth, and has, finally, circumnavigated the globe itself. He has, by these means, transmitted to one region the arts of life discovered in another, so that each one has profited by the improvements of the rest.

The vegetable world also offers a boundless field for the exercise of human industry. From this source he obtains the largest supply of his food, which is derived from the seeds of one tribe of plants, the leaves of another, and the roots of a third. From the juices of several plants he obtains what, of all sweets, is the most grateful to the human palate; from others, wine and beer, tea, coffee, and chocolate, to cheer and nourish his nervous system. Of the trees of the forest he constructs houses, ships, carriages, household furniture, and utensils in endless variety. From one plant he obtains the materials for light clothing at a less expense than from any other source. From vegetables he derives dyes of every hue, and medicines for the cure or mitigation of every disease. By means of ingenious mill machinery, he makes running water, or the stream, pulverize one set of vegetables into flour, spin another into thread, and then weave it into cloth, press out the oil from the olive, cider from the apple, separate cotton from its seed, and convert trees into planks. He transforms flax and hemp into lines and ropes, as well as cloth; and in a considerable portion of the fabrics of human art, mineral, animal, and vegetable substances have been combined to produce them. Thus a ship, a coach, a piano, and a book are the joint result of all three; and even a pair of boots has commonly the same threefold origin.

As, in civilized society, human labor and skill are principally employed either in producing the raw materials, or in giving to those materials new forms, suited to the uses of man, or in transporting either those materials or manufactures from place to place, all industrious employments have been divided into 1. Those of agriculture, mining, and fishing; 2. Those of manufactures, and 3. Those of commerce; which we will now successively notice.

CHAPTER VIII.

AGRICULTURAL INDUSTRY.

When the cultivation of the earth was first resorted to for the purpose of meeting the wants of an increasing population, agriculture was naturally rude and imperfect, compared with what it afterwards became. The labor by which it was then carried on was probably that of the retainers about the large proprietors, as we have seen in the clans of Scotland. A part of this labor found employment in the culture of the soil, and a part in the practice of arts which were suited to their humble skill and the simple wants of their employers. They were smiths, tailors, wrights, and masons; and they being designated by their occupations, these became the most common surnames.

But this mode of culture, equally unfavorable to a large production and a frugal consumption, was not likely to last; and, from the pressure of increasing numbers, some of these retainers, whether employed in husbandry or handicraft, would seek independent homes by renting small tracts from their former employer. At first, from the abundance of land compared with the population, the tenant would receive nearly all the produce that he made; but since, from the increase of numbers, the value of that produce would, as we have seen, be steadily rising, the remuneration of labor would as steadily diminish.

It is laid down by some theorists that, in consequence of the admitted rise of raw produce, in the progress of society, the wages of labor, which must be sufficient to support the laborer, must also rise. But this is a contradiction. The only sense in which raw produce can be said to rise, is that it will exchange for more labor, which is the same thing as saying that labor has fallen. It is then a fundamental law of society, that raw produce, in the progress of increase of numbers, tends to increase in value, and labor to diminish. They both are the consequences of the same change in the demand and supply of labor and its means of subsistence; for by the continual increase of population, and the limited quantity of land, labor becomes gradually cheaper by its increased supply, and raw produce dearer by the increased demand for it. Thus we find labor to be cheaper in China than in Europe, and cheaper in Europe than America, while raw produce has in those countries a correspondent dearness.

The source of this error is the supposition that the laborer's subsistence is a fixed quantity; but this subsistence is susceptible of great variation. It is true that the food consumed does not admit of much reduction in the *quantity*, consistent with the physical well-being of the individual, but it makes a great difference in its *value,* whether that food is animal or vegetable, and whether it is of one species of vegetable or another. A man may consume animal food liberally or sparingly; he may subsist chiefly on bread made of wheat, rye, or oats, or lastly, on potatoes. The same portion of soil will support a greater or less number of human beings as they subsist on one or the other of these aliments. The difference may be that a square mile would support 80 persons who consume animal food abundantly; 120 persons who consume it sparingly; 160 or 180, when they subsist chiefly on grain; and from 300 to 400, when they subsist on potatoes. As population advances, and the means of subsistence become comparatively more difficult of attainment, a portion of the community must pass from a dearer to a cheaper mode of subsistence, or the population must become stationary. Past experience seems to show that when this alternative is presented, the multiplying propensity will prevail, and the cheaper mode of subsistence be resorted to.

From the preceding views it follows that, in the earlier stages of society, both raw produce, and the fabrics of human labor and ingenuity, are obtained with difficulty. In the second stage they are both plentiful, especially raw produce. In the third stage the laborer can obtain manufactures with more ease, but raw produce with increased difficulty. The people of Europe, during the middle ages, were in the first stage. The people of the United States have always been in the second stage; and the European nations are now in the third.

The decline in the remuneration of labor, incidental to the third stage, though so probable, and in accordance with the past history of mankind, seems not to be inevitable. England, by means of her extensive commerce, the excellence of her manufactures, and her system of colonial monopoly, has given such additional value to the labor of her people, as greatly to retard its fall of price with the increase of population. But there is a more general and certain mode of preventing the reduction of the laborer's wages below the rate of comfortable subsistence. This is what Malthus calls the preventive or prudential check to redundant numbers, and which he considers is rather to be wished than expected.

There is some ground for the hope that the high standard of comfort which has ever existed in the United States may prove a timely and efficient check to a redundant population; and this gratifying view derives support from that high degree of self-respect which is a natural consequence of our form of government, and which is felt by the humblest of our citizens.

A fact disclosed by the census of 1840, and confirmed by that of 1850, is calculated to encourage those hopes. It shows a steady diminution of the number of children in the United States under ten years of age, compared with the women; and, although this result may possibly be owing to a greater mortality of the children, or to less prolificness of the women, yet neither of these facts is to be presumed without evidence; and the most rational explanation of the fact is to suppose a short postponement of the average age at which females marry. It is for time to show whether this diminution in the number of children has been produced by a change of manners, which has its limit, or by causes that will continue to act, so that our population will not pass, or much exceed, their present high standard of subsistence.

In this gradual reduction of the wages of labor, when population is checked neither by the self-restraining prudence of individuals nor by great public calamities, what is the lowest point to which those wages can descend without lessening the numbers of the community?

Until those numbers have reached the level of the means of subsistence, the lowest wages to which competition can reduce the laborer will be enough to support himself and a family of an average number in the ordinary mode of subsistence. But when that level is reached, as in China, then the limit may descend still lower, until the wages become barely sufficient to support the laborer himself. In such a community, incapable of further increase, the loss by death is repaired principally by the richer classes, whose natural multiplication may be the same, or nearly the same, as where population was thin; and from this stock the laboring class will be ever receiving fresh supplies. It thus appears that, while the maximum of the wages of agricultural labor is all the raw produce which the laborer can make after paying the expense of cultivation, but no rent, the minimum is no more than is necessary for his subsistence. At this meagre rate it is believed that labor can always be procured in China, Hindostan, and other parts of Asia.

In treating of agricultural labor, it is proper to notice *Slavery*, which prevails in nearly one-half of the States of this Union, and which is viewed with very different sentiments by those two great local divisions.

By one party it is thus impugned: a most obvious consequence of this condition is, that where ordinary labor is performed by slaves, such labor, by a natural association, is regarded as beneath the dignity of free men, and they are consequently thus rendered indolent and idle. Nor is this all: the slave, not being stimulated to industry by the expectation of receiving the fruits of his own labor, is likely, from the love of ease so natural to man, to work less willingly, with less energy, and to avoid toil when he can. To counteract this propensity, superintendents are necessary, who sometimes resort to punishment to compel that labor, which with freemen is readily and voluntarily exerted from self-interest. The cost of such superintendence is therefore a charge on agriculture from which free communities are exempt; and compulsion, moreover, can scarcely ever make the labor of a slave as productive as that of the free man.

The instinctive feelings of the slave, it is further urged, also impel him to extraordinary expense and waste. He is therefore generally thievish, careless, and improvident. Slavery has thus been said to consign one-half of the community in the Southern States to unwilling labor, and the other half either to idleness, or, for preventing ennui, to vicious indulgences.

Such are the theoretical objections to domestic slavery; and yet there are many facts which are at variance with this theory, so as to compel those who are in pursuit of truth to make large deductions from the conclusions to which the mere speculators on this subject have been generally conducted.

Thus, as to the unproductiveness of slave labor: after the emancipation of the slaves in the English West Indies, the labor of that class was greatly diminished, and the confident predictions of the abolitionists were completely falsified, as the products of those islands, when cultivated by freemen, was far less than when cultivated by slaves. In Jamaica, much the largest island, the falling off was the greatest. The negroes, finding it practicable to procure the small patches of ground which, in that genial soil and climate, are sufficient for their support, have mainly withdrawn themselves from the toilsome and irksome labor of making sugar, and can be tempted to continue it only by working at high wages, a few hours of the day, and certain days of the week; so that an able-bodied laborer now produces scarce a third or a fourth of what he formerly earned In Barbadoes, indeed, where the population is very dense, necessity compels the mass of the negroes to work on the plantations as formerly, and the produce of this island has not diminished, but has even increased. Between these extremes the other islands were found, some yielding far less than their former product, and others approaching it. Of late, by the aid of the Coolies, whom the Government has introduced into its sugar colonies at a great expense, the present product of all of them except Jamaica is equal to what it formerly was.

In the slaveholding States of this Union there are some persons who, brought up among slaves, have acquired so much skill in managing them, that the products of their labor are scarcely inferior to those of freemen. Proprietors of this description excite emulation among the slaves, and make use of small indulgences and rewards as incentives to their industry, which are more efficient than those of punishment, inasmuch as the former make them identify their master's interest with their own, and consider themselves, in fact, as members of the same patriarchal family. These cases of the judicious and successful management of slaves are not, indeed, of common occurrence, but they are sufficient to show how much the evils of slavery are capable of mitigation.

There are also some social benefits growing out of this institution which it is proper to state, to pass for what they are worth. The habit of command, to which the master of slaves has been familiarized from his infancy, peculiarly fits him for many of the higher duties of civilized life. He is thus likely to be better qualified for exercising authority both in the army and navy, and even in the civil department. It is, perhaps, thus that the Southern States have furnished more than their proportion of those who have held the higher offices of the government.

The institution seems to be also favorable to manners, by giving that quiet ease which the habitual self-respect of the slaveholder is so likely to bestow; so that the manners of the cultivated classes in the slaveholding States differ little or nothing from those of people of rank in Europe.

On the other hand, slavery has been thought to beget overbearing manners, and to have an unpropitious influence on the temper. This opinion, which seems plausible, was adopted by Mr. Jefferson, and he has given currency to the hypothesis by the weight of his authority. Yet when we find that it is not confirmed by the touchstone of fact; and that, if our public men are regarded as fair specimens of the population of their respective States, those of the South may well compare with those of the North for mildness, clemency, and amenity, then we are bound to consider speculative opinions, which are thus forcibly opposed, as among the fallacies of ingenious theory. There could be no better refutation of this specious philosophy than Mr. Jefferson himself.

It may be further remarked that since our country contains numbers of the African race, so great as to be beyond the power of removal, and since they are universally regarded by the whites as inferior to themselves, both physically and intellectually, the Southern States are irreconcilably averse to the emancipation of their slaves. But, in the meanwhile, it may be fairly questioned whether that portion of the proscribed race who are in bondage are not as well cared for, and in fact as happy, as their brethren in the Northern States, where they are free, but where they are not treated with the same easy familiarity and kindness as by Southern gentlemen, and where the mutual affection and good will which often subsist between the white and the colored man are unknown.

These remarks are made, not to show that slavery, as some have maintained, is a positive good, but simply to indicate that here, as in all human concerns, evil and good are closely intermingled, and that, to come to just conclusions, we must make a fair estimate of both.

But an important question here presents itself—Is domestic slavery to be regarded as a permanent institution in the United States? To this I do not hesitate to return an answer in the negative; and to assert that, as serfdom, which once existed in every part of Europe, has there universally disappeared, except in Russia, where it gives indications that before long it will entirely cease, it must, from the same general causes, also terminate in the United States.

We have seen that, in the progress of society, after the more fertile lands are all occupied, the price of labor will decline with the increasing density of population. Now, long before that density has reached its maximum, the price of labor will have so fallen that the value of a slave will not repay the cost of rearing him; in which case, slavery, no longer profitable to the master, will naturally expire.

The large extent of fertile lands in the United States still unoccupied, together with the present thinness of their population, may at first lead to the supposition that the period adverted to, when our lands will be less able to furnish an easy subsistence to the people, is removed to an indefinite distance—not less than several centuries. An easy calculation will, however, lead us to a very different result. Supposing our present population to be 30,000,000—and it is probably more; then in three duplications it will be (30 × 2 = 60 × 2 = 120 × 2 =) 240,000,000;

which would give for our whole territory an average population of seventy to the square mile.

The average period of our doubling during the seventy years from 1790 to 1850 was less than twenty-four years. Let us, however, suppose that the first period from this time would be twenty-five years, the second twenty-six years, and the third twenty-seven years — making, in all, seventy-eight years, to the year 1937, when our numbers would be 240,000,000.

Though we have no certain and precise data for determining at what degree of density the value of slaves would not repay the cost of rearing them, yet it seems probable, from the condition of Europe when villainage there terminated,* that a density much less than seventy to the square mile is inconsistent with slavery. But should even a greater density be assumed as the limit, that limit, by the

---

In 1843, in a work on the census, I hazarded the opinion, founded on such imperfect information as I possessed, that, in a period of from about sixty to eighty years, slavery would probably expire in the United States. They soon afterwards obtained an accession of territory of more than 800,000 square miles (Texas and part of Mexico), which, by lessening the density of population, would postpone the period. It would not, however, put it off for more than ten years; and, on a revision of the views then taken, I see no reason to change them, and still think that, in less than a hundred years from that time, slavery will, in all, or nearly all, of the States, die a natural and an easy death.

uncontrollable laws of human multiplication, must be eventually reached.

The subsequent rise in the price of slaves has strangely seemed to some a contradiction to the hypothesis of the spontaneous termination of slavery. But there is no inconsistency in the two facts. The price of slaves is high in consequence of the profits of their labor in making cotton, and of the peculiar fitness of the soil and climate of the Southern States for the culture of that commodity; and so long as the supply does not exceed the demand, the prices both of cotton and slaves must continue high. But those prices must be seriously affected by the further increase of slaves. By the census of 1850, their number exceeded 3,000,000. It is probably now near 4,000,000; but whatever it may be, in twenty-five years it will have doubled, in fifty years have quadrupled, and of course be able to produce four times as much cotton, tobacco, and other agricultural produce as at present. But in that time the consumers of cotton and tobacco in Europe and this country will not have doubled, and consequently the supply will be proportionally reduced. There will be no reason at that period why the making of cotton should be better rewarded than any other agricultural labor—the price of which will have undergone, from its increased supply, a general fall, and a part of it be compelled to seek employment in manufactures, as has been previously explained.

Let us now glance at some of the diversities of human labor in different countries. Man, ever compelled to more or less exertion for his subsistence, is no where so industrious as in the Temperate Zones. There, work is often a pleasure as well as a business; and active exercise, both of body and mind, is a want of his nature. In the polar regions he cannot always endure the intense cold, and, in the season when he can work, he has a very limited field for profitable employment. The chilled earth makes no return to the husbandman, and the inhabitant has little occupation but in the precarious toils of the hunter or fisherman. In the Torrid Zone, where the soil, under a heat that never intermits, is most prolific, labor is peculiarly irksome, and is fortunately little needed. There, too, man is less disposed to consume animal food, the more expensive species of aliment; and the bounty of nature furnishes so ample a store from the vegetable kingdom, that he can subsist upon the product of one-fourth, or even less, of the area required to support him in the Temperate Zones.

Besides these effects of climate on human labor, moral causes have also much influence. One of the most potent of these influences is that of government. Where the rights of property are accurately defined and efficiently protected, as they are in free countries, there men are likely to be industrious from the expectation of enjoying the fruits of their industry. This is the case in the United States, in England,

and, in a less degree, in most other parts of Europe. But where a despotic and rapacious government appropriates to its own purposes most of the earnings of the people, there less will be produced, and the product will be less economically used. Such is the condition of nearly all the countries of Asia; yet the pressing wants of the dense numbers of China force the people there to a high degree of industry, by which the evils of an over-crowded population are greatly mitigated.

In Spain, Portugal, and Italy, the people are far less industrious than they are in England, France, and Germany. This inferiority may be in part ascribed to the difference of climate, and partly to the difference in the amount of civil freedom.

Education also here exerts a benignant influence. It tends to make men more moral and provident, and less prone to idleness and intemperance. The general diffusion of mental instruction throughout New England has doubtless contributed to the great and diversified industry which characterizes the people of that part of the Union.

It is by agricultural industry that much the larger part of raw produce is furnished. From this source is derived the principal portion of human aliment, both vegetable and animal. Wheat, maize, rice, rye, barley, buckwheat; every kind of pulse and potatoes, and other roots; beef, mutton, pork, and every species of poultry; wool, skins, and hides; cotton, hemp, flax, and tobacco; indigo, and other dye-stuffs. But large supplies are also furnished from mines, as coal, the ores of metals, marble, stone, and other minerals. The ocean, rivers, and lakes, likewise contribute their portion in fish and fish-oil, oysters, and other shell-fish.

In addition to the before-mentioned species of raw produce, there are many commodities important to human comfort, and extensively consumed, which are equally the product of agricultural industry and of that which we are about to consider.

CHAPTER IX.

MANUFACTURING INDUSTRY.

Of the three great employments of national industry, that of giving to raw produce the forms adapted to the purposes of man, or of manufactures, requires the most manual adroitness. In this talent there is a great diversity among individuals, so that some are able to do as much in an hour as others can in twice or thrice the time, and not seldom perform operations to which most others are incompetent. There is, indeed, in every mechanical employment, as in the nicer productions of art, as great a difference in the goodness of the work, as in the celerity with which it has been produced. Hence, some acquire reputation as bootmakers, tailors, hatters, or as makers of fine cutlery, cabinet-work, watches, or jewelry. Even in the simple operations of making nails or bricks, the labor of some is twice as efficient as that of others.

But the greatest advantage possessed by manufactures in the employment of labor is, that they admit the co-operation of several individuals in the same object, by which the product is so greatly multiplied. This was first noticed by Adam Smith, under the designation of the "division of labor," and was strikingly illustrated by him in the manufacture of pins. If one person was to perform all the operations required for the fabrication of this little implement, he could not make twenty pins in a day—perhaps not more than one; but by distributing these several operations among a dozen or twenty workmen, the proportional number to each one would be upwards of 4000 pins in a day.

This prodigious gain is referred by Smith to three circumstances: the increased adroitness and rapidity of execution acquired in the performance of a single act; the saving of time which would be lost when a workman passes from one operation to another, which perchance is to be executed in another place, as well as with other tools; and lastly, machinery may be more extensively substituted for human labor in proportion as the operation is more simple.

The gain from the last-mentioned source may be illustrated by some striking examples. The machine which makes wool or cotton cards has saved an immense amount of human labor, that was previously expended in forming its little wire-hooks, one by one, and, by the same slow process, inserting them in a piece of leather perforated to receive each hook. At present, the machine cuts the wire to a proper length; bends it into a hook; perforates the leather—at the same time inserting the hook, until the card is complete. All this occupies so little time, that the card is then sold for a small part of what it had formerly cost.

But of all labor-saving machines, the cotton-gin, in a national point of view, is the most important. Before it was invented, the seed of that species of cotton which can alone be cultivated in the interior portion of the United States, was separated from the fibrous part by the human fingers; by which operation one person could clean not more than a pound a day. Thus furnished in such small quantity, it was valueless as an export, and was used only to a moderate extent for manufactures in the Southern States. But after Whitney's invention of the *saw-gin*—a combination of circular saws and brushes, the simplest moving-power—a small stream, or a horse, was made to perform this work at an insignificant expense, so as to render cotton a general article of culture, where the climate permitted its growth, until it became an export of more value than that of all other commodities combined.

The manufacture of cotton into cloth has received improvement as great as has the production of the raw material. The inventions which have been made in England for carding, spinning, and weaving cotton by machinery, have so facilitated the manufacture of this material, that they have contributed as much as the cotton-gin to the cheapness of its fabrics; and, by their joint operation, a large proportion of those fabrics now sell for one-sixth or one-eighth part of their former cost. All the operations of manufacturing cotton-cloth, which were once performed by human hands, are now done, and better done, by machines, which are put in motion by running water, or steam, or horses; and the consumption has been so extended by its cheapness, that it now gives profitable employment to a far greater number of persons than ever.

The machinery which has so lessened the cost of cotton fabrics has been also applied to those of wool and of linen, but not to the same extent, nor with the same advantage.

When, in political economy, labor is considered to be of uniform value, it refers only to labor in its simplest form — that of an ordinary man, exercised with ordinary skill. But in truth, there is no merchantable commodity which varies in value more than human labor; and it is proper to notice the sources of this diversity.

First. The difference of skill which an employment may require. The superiority may consist either in manual dexterity, as in the case of a mechanic, or in professional knowledge, as in the case of a lawyer or physician, or of both united, as in the case of a surgeon; and it is immaterial whether the skill be the result of previous instruction, or the endowment of nature.

In many branches of industry, the most toilsome portions of the labor expended are of the cheapest kind, while another portion, requiring extraordinary skill, finds its remuneration only in a very high price. Thus the first preparation of a piece of marble for a statue may be performed by an ordinary stone-cutter, at the low wages of common labor; but the last part of the process of making such intractable material closely copy the diversified forms of animal life may command twenty, or even fifty times as much remuneration. So of the finest piece of work in watchmaking, and the manufacture of plate or jewelry.

Secondly. The price of labor varies, also, according to the greater or less agreeableness of the operation. In the same degree that an employment is distasteful, its compensation must be higher, to counterbalance the disadvantage. Hence the office of an executioner, which is naturally revolting to the feelings, and is therefore held in great aversion or contempt, is commonly very well rewarded. This odium has probably suggested those machines which have been devised to execute the dread sentence of the law without the visible agency of man, as the *maiden* in Scotland, and the *guillotine* in France. The business of negro-trading is also one which is generally odious, as violating the dictates of humanity, and as implying a want of human sympathy. To compensate this unpopularity, the trade is very profitable. The great gains of the African slave trade long avowedly prevented its abolition by the British Government. Even now they are often sufficient to defy the hostility of the principal maritime powers of the world.

There are some trades which are held by popular sentiment in disrespect, as requiring less manly quali ties, or as subjecting their followers to menial services; such are those of barbers and tailors. The profits of their labor, which is comparatively light, are enhanced by these disparaging circumstances. On the other hand, the occupation of a soldier, which is often one of toil, and always one of danger, has commonly but a small pecuniary reward; but the honor and glory associated with this employment constitute a part of its remuneration.

The small compensation which clerical men often receive arises partly from the high respect in which their profession is held, and partly from the influence which it gives to clergymen over the minds of so many of their respective congregations. A similar regard to honor and power often induces a lawyer to accept the office of a judge, with a salary of less than half of his former professional gains, though the lighter labors of his new occupation may have also exerted some influence. We see the same principle operating on militia offices, in which there is generally not only no emolument received, but a certain expense incurred, in the purchase of an uniform, epaulettes, and other trappings of office.

In countries in which there is a privileged class, the honor of belonging to it is deemed a very high reward. The rank of a peer, in monarchial countries, and even that which is merely personal, as the post of a knight of the garter, are by many estimated beyond a large pecuniary pension. James II. raised a considerable sum of money by appealing to this desire of distinction in the sale of baronetcies. The sum paid for the honor was about $5000—equivalent, in the scale of wealth, to more than $10,000 at the present day.

Some occupations receive higher rewards in consequence of the dangers to which they are exposed. Thus those who work in mines, from the dreadful explosions that there occasionally occur, receive high wages. So do those who are employed in working steam-engines. The compensation to ordinary seamen would also be augmented by its dangers as well as its hardships, if their occupation were not attractive to the young and adventurous by reason of those very dangers; and if it were not afterwards pursued by the force of habit, and because the seafaring life in a great measure unfits its followers for other employments.

Thirdly. The moral qualities required for the competent discharge of some employments have an influence on their compensation. Wherever integrity is essential to the faithful exercise of their duties, the remuneration is proportionally high. Hence the liberal pay which is given to public functionaries, according to their responsibility, and the confidence reposed in them. So of those who are entrusted with the safekeeping of money. The frequent instances which have occurred in our country of abuses of such trusts, by bank-officers and others, seems to show that the rewards paid to honesty have been below the standard which justice and policy would prescribe.*

The effect of moral qualities in raising the pay of services which confer no special honor, is seen in the remuneration received by superintendents and overseers. As the value of their services depends mainly on an unremitting circumspection, and a close as well as honest attention to little things, which qualities are found by experience to be rare, they are proportionally well rewarded; and one overseer of a plantation or farm can as easily obtain a salary of $800, or even $1000, as another can obtain one of $200.

Fourthly. The irregularity or unsteadiness of an employment tends to raise its remuneration. When a trade can be carried on only at particular seasons, its wages must be sufficient to compensate for the time unemployed. Thus a bricklayer, or plasterer, who cannot work in very cold weather, must have

---

* It was a memorable saying of a former Treasurer of Virginia, on resigning his office, that "he trusted he had quitted it with clean hands, as he certainly did with empty ones." He was indeed of unimpeachable integrity, but his last remark took away much of the merit claimed by the first, since it is only *full* hands which, on such occasions, are likely to be soiled.

higher wages than a carpenter, who can work at all seasons. Hence, their pay, which may be different by the day, may be the same in the year. The labors of some professional men are doubtless better rewarded for the time they are unemployed. The same circumstances increase the remuneration of undertakers, musicians, and of all whose services are required only on rare occasions.

Fifthly. The probability or improbability of success in an employment has a proportional effect on its rewards. In some trades, which at once minister to the ordinary wants of mankind, and are of easy acquisition, an ordinary degree of industry is certain to be successful. But where they minister to the wants of only a few, or require peculiar talents, failure is more common than success, and the rewards of the small number who are successful are the greater from the diminution of the competitors. Hence the high remuneration which is occasionally received by some lawyers, physicians, and surgeons. The prizes which they have drawn in the lottery of life may be nearly equal to the losses of those who have failed.

But they are probably never quite equal. It has been observed that the uncertainty of success in any sort of business or employment, though it does enhance its remuneration in the way just mentioned, commonly does so to a less extent than that to which it seems to be justly entitled. The reason is that the occasional high rewards—like high prizes which have been drawn in lotteries—have more effect in attracting competitors than the failures have in lessening their number. The extraordinary gains now and then made in a new branch of commerce, are sure to be followed by others with a reckless eagerness which often terminates in bankruptcy and ruin. The large income obtained by one lawyer or physician out of fifty, is thus a main cause of these professions being so over-stocked.

All these facts show the undue predominance of hope in our estimates of the future. Wherever, then, the profits of an employment are occasionally large, but precarious, they are certain to be over-rated, and consequently to be over-crowded with competitors; while, on the other hand, those occupations in which the gains are gradual and moderate, are more certain, and above the general average. Hence it is that there is a larger proportion of fortunes made, and fewer failures, in the business of a butcher, baker, tanner, or grocer, than in that of a great ship-owner, or merchant, engaged in foreign commerce.

In all these modifications of the rewards of labor, we see the governing influence of the law of supply and demand; and that every circumstance which has been mentioned as either increasing or diminishing those rewards, has done so by lessening or augmenting the supply of labor required, and thus affecting the demand, or number of competitors.

Sixthly. The five preceding modes of influencing the price of labor are substantially those laid down by Adam Smith, who first introduced them to the notice of the political economist. But there is yet another, in which the anomalous reward received for labor falls under neither of those five classes, and which can be referred only to *custom*. Thus, in the State of Maryland, it is usual to give large gratuitous fees to the clerk who issues marriage-licenses, while, in most of the States, extra fees are given on such occasions only to the officiating clergyman. In the city of Washington, it is the usage, on the death of a member of Congress, for each hackney-coach in the city to attend the funeral procession, for which service, instead of the ordinary fare of fifty cents, five dollars is always paid. There are also settled fees for certain professional services, which are commonly very disproportionate to the time and skill exerted. As these rewards of labor exceed the ordinary average, they naturally tend to increase the number of competitors, and, by a correspondent lessening of profits, restore the just equilibrium between wages and labor.

In all manufactures there are three elements which combine to determine the market value of the finished fabric. These are the raw material, the labor, and the machinery; and they occupy very different proportions in different species of manufactures. Thus, in cotton fabrics, in which the labor is performed chiefly by machinery, and is, consequently, cheaper, the raw material is by much the most valuable part.

In those of wool, the raw material is also the most costly, but the value of the labor and machinery expended approaches that of the raw material.

In those of iron, there is a very great diversity, according to the character of the fabric. In small articles, such as needles, watch-springs, and the like, the cost of the raw material is insignificant; but in anchors, pieces of ordnance, and the iron bars of a railway, it exceeds that of the labor and machinery.

In manufactures of leather, the value of the labor and of the raw material are generally nearly equal.

In silk manufactures, the material, which is itself the result of much human labor and manipulation, is always an important element; but in its most costly fabrics, labor is by far the largest element, as in the Gobelin tapestry, velvets, and rich brocades.

In all manufactures of pottery and glass, the raw material is of little value, except in making porcelain; when the kaolin earth, which is found in few places, is brought from a great distance. There is a vein of this material extending through the States of Delaware, Maryland, and Virginia, which will doubtless one day give rise to extensive factories of its beautiful wares.

In the manufacture of books, the cost of the principal material, paper, is proportionally small; but the paper itself has been fabricated of old rags, some pounds of which, costing but a few cents, when converted into a book, may sell, in consequence of the labor bestowed on it, for as many dollars. The very coarse paper made of oakum, or old hempen rope, is manufactured into various articles of *papier maché* of great beauty and cost.

But it will be no long time before the United States must of necessity fabricate its own manufactures. They cannot always derive their chief supplies, as at present, from foreign countries.

Commerce, we know, is an exchange of equivalents — of domestic for foreign products. Such an exchange is indispensable to its existence. At present, we obtain all our fine manufactures, and part of the coarse ones, in return for our agricultural products sent abroad. But this commerce will be greatly modified by our increase of population. Our present numbers are 30,000,000; which, in fifty years, by two duplications, will be 120,000,000. They will consequently then need manufactures to four times their present amount, which will require a correspondent increase of our exports.

It may doubtless be perfectly competent for the workshops of Europe to furnish this fourfold supply, but how is it to be paid for? Will Europe be then able to purchase four times as much cotton, and tobacco, and other products of our agriculture? That is not to be supposed. The consumption of cotton seems, of all those products, to be the most susceptible of a great increase; and yet it would seem extravagant to estimate the increased consumption at one hundred per cent. But, admitting this twofold increase, we could obtain in this way only half of our required supply of manufactures, and employ only half the proportion of our agricultural labor that is employed at present, since cotton and tobacco will not be made beyond the existing market for them. The labor thus spared from agriculture will naturally be employed to meet the increased demand for manufactures. Commerce being no longer able to furnish these in sufficiency, we shall manufacture for ourselves.

The change here adverted to will be gradual. But even in twenty-four or twenty-five years, when our demands for manufactures will have doubled, the foreign market for our agricultural products may have increased in a much smaller proportion, by reason of the moderate increase of the population of Europe in that time, and consequently a part of the labor now employed in agriculture will have been even then diverted to manufactures.

There are several commodities of great utility and extensive consumption which have equal claims to be regarded as raw produce, and as the product of manufacturing industry. Of this character is sugar, whether made from the cane, the beet, or the maple. So of every kind of wine, of cider, of butter and cheese, and vegetable oils. Salt is also as much a product of mining as of manufacturing industry, as is also bar-iron, and other metallic products.

CHAPTER X.

COMMERCIAL INDUSTRY.

DIFFERENT countries, in consequence of diversities of climate or soil, produce useful articles in peculiar abundance and cheapness; and occasionally produce commodities that some regions cannot produce at all. Thus we get tea from China; coffee from Hayti, Brazil, or Arabia; wine from France, Spain, Portugal, or their colonies. There is a similar diversity in the products of human labor. We obtain our cutlery, hardware, and most of our woollens, from England; our silks from France and China; our linen from Germany and Ireland. In our own country, tobacco, cotton, timber, and naval stores, are more abundant and cheap than in any other. Every country, then, by exchanging those commodities which are there cheapest for those which are dearer, as it may do by its foreign traffic, is a gainer — and hence are the profits of COMMERCE.

Thus, in Turks Island, where, in consequence of a dry climate and hot sun, salt is made from sea-water by natural evaporation, it is so cheap that from five to ten bushels of it are equal in value to only one bushel of Indian corn; and there are many parts of the United States in which a bushel of salt has the value of four or five bushels of corn. So in the West Indies, an hundred pounds of flour will often be of equal value with two hundred pounds of sugar; while in this country, an hundred pounds of sugar may be equivalent to two hundred pounds of flour. By an exchange, then, of the salt for the corn, in one case, or the flour for the sugar, in the other, each country obtains the dearer foreign commodity in return for its own cheaper product; which exchange commonly affords to both parties a fair return, and sometimes a very liberal one, for the trouble and expense of the transportation.

As this expense of carriage is the principal cause of the different values which the same article bears in different places, whatever facilitates and cheapens the cost of transport, in the same degree adds to the productiveness of the national industry. Hence the importance of shipping for commerce with distant countries, and of canals and railroads for domestic commerce. If, for instance, the transport of a ton to a given distance, by any one of these modes, was a dollar, and, by some improvement, the cost could be reduced one-half, then of course there would be, on all commodities transported that distance, fifty cents saved to the producers or consumers, and which would commonly be divided between them.

Improvements in transportation enlarge the sphere of the market, as well as better that which previously existed. Thus, in the case supposed (the reduction of the cost of carriage from a dollar to fifty cents), the field of transport, and consequently of traffic, may be extended twice as far, and obtain the benefit of all the additional markets comprehended within the greater distance.

We have a ready illustration of the contributions of commerce to our comforts in an ordinary breakfast. The table is probably made of mahogany brought from Hayti or Honduras. The cloth which covers it, or the napkins, were the product of Ireland or Germany. The tea came from China; the coffee from Batavia, or Brazil; the sugar from the West Indies, or Louisiana; the knives from England, with handles of ivory from Africa; the spoons and forks, and other articles of silver, from Mexico; the plates, cups, and saucers, from China, England, or France; the salt from Liverpool, and the pepper from India; the meat, fish, or eggs, butter and bread, being the only domestic products. Thus, all the four quarters of the world had contributed materials to this daily meal, employing some eight or ten ships, navigating many thousands of miles, and hundreds, or perhaps thousands, of individuals in their transportation. If we examine our ordinary apparel, or the furniture of our houses, we shall, in like manner, find that a considerable part has been afforded by the exchanges of commerce.*

* Some years after the preceding illustration had formed a part of my lectures in the University, a similar exposition appeared in one of the English Reviews. It has doubtless occurred to others.

That portion of the mercantile class who carry on the foreign commerce of the country, commonly employ large capitals, by which they occasionally enrich themselves by benefiting the community. But, as their trade is very irregular, sometimes yielding enormous profits, and sometimes being attended with loss, the average gains of this employment of capital, according to a rule previously adverted to, is probably less than those of most others.

There is another portion of the same class who are employed in dividing larger quantities of useful commodities into small parcels, to suit the various wants of different members of the community, for which they obtain a higher price to compensate them for their trouble, for the deterioration which many articles experience by the keeping, and for the time that they may remain unsold. These are retail dealers and shop-keepers. Their business being less precarious than that of the importing merchant, is less likely to be followed by bankruptcy, and is rewarded by greater average profits.

There are some dealers of this class in whom integrity is of peculiar importance. In most of the commodities in which they deal, there are various qualities, differing greatly in value, which are not always discerned by any, and not at all by the inexperienced. These dealers, then, supposing them honest in the price or measure of their wares, may impose on their customers as to the *quality* with impunity. Of this description are grocers, dealers in liquor, and druggists.

The gains of foreign commerce have been estimated by very different rules. It was once considered that a commerce in which the imports exceeded the exports in value was injurious, and was beneficial only when the exports predominated; it being assumed that the difference was paid in gold and silver, which were deemed more desirable than any other commodity, and thought to constitute the only just measure of the national wealth. Governments accordingly discouraged imports by heavy duties, and sometimes even by prohibitions, and encouraged exports by bounties and drawbacks, or the repayment of duties.

This course of policy, called *the mercantile system*, involved more than one error. It was a mistake to suppose that there was any peculiar advantage in receiving the precious metals, or peculiar disadvantage in paying them away, when the free course of trade required it; any extraordinary value which they might chance to have beyond merchandize justly determining in each case the expediency or inexpediency of exporting them.

It is also a mistake to assume that the excess of the exports over the imports always indicated the profits of a trade. It was, for example, formerly not unusual for an adventurer in some Atlantic city to take out to the Pacific such articles as were suited to the trade with the natives on that coast, to the amount of a few thousand dollars. These articles were in due time exchanged with the Indians for furs, which, being then transported to China, were there converted into a cargo of teas and other Chinese goods, worth, when brought to the United States, one or two hundred thousand dollars. Thus a trade was established by which the goods exported had brought a return of perhaps an hundred times their cost, and which was, consequently, as gainful as, by the prevalent doctrine of the balance of trade, it would have been pronounced injurious. In like manner a ship is fitted for a whaling voyage, and takes out nothing but provisions for the crew, with her fishing tackle, and in a year, or two, returns with a cargo of oil and spermaceti, worth perhaps an hundred thousand dollars.

These, however, are anomalous cases, and tend to make us overrate the errors of the rule for ascertaining the balance of trade. If, indeed, all imported merchandise was paid for by the exports in the same branch of business, as in the two cases mentioned, then the reverse of the old rule would be correct, and a trade would be profitable in proportion as the value of the imports exceeded that of the exports. But such is not the fact; and the excess of imports may indicate not the profits to the importer, but the amount of debt contracted by him.

In a series of years, indeed, the whole amount of imports and of exports are of equal value, with the exception of a small excess in the value of imports; inasmuch as nations, like individuals, in their exchanges, commonly receive more value than they part with. But occasionally there is a great difference of value between the two. Now, the exports of a country may commonly be regarded as so much sold to foreign nations, and the imports as so much bought from them. But, if a country buys more than it sells, this is *prima facie* evidence that it is living too fast. It so far lessens the national wealth, and contracts a debt which it may not be able to discharge without inconvenience, and even embarrassment.

Such is often the condition of the United States in its commerce with Great Britain, which constitutes three-fourths of their trade with the world. In every flush of prosperity they increase their imports of foreign merchandise, and are but too apt to continue their extra consumption when their extra means have ceased. The abundant capital of Great Britain enables our merchants to obtain credit whenever they ask it, and the debt thus contracted lays the foundation for future embarrassment. These facts seem to present a yet stronger ground for a tolerably high impost than does the encouragement of domestic industry, as it would tend to check unwarranted expense of living; and so far as it failed in introducing frugality, it would draw from the improvident class some compensation to the public, and strengthen the nation in its ability to encounter the difficulties of debt.

There are many fabrics extensively consumed, particularly those of iron, wool, cotton, and leather, which are partly manufactured at home and partly obtained from abroad by the exchanges of commerce; and this diversity of origin, differently affecting different interests, has given rise to a question of public policy which has warmly agitated the community; and the controversy has been the more serious and threatening from the fact that the principal parties were separated by geographical lines — the Northern States, which take the lead in manufactures, being in favor of protecting and encouraging that branch of industry by taxing its foreign rivals; while the Southern States, which are mere consumers of manufactured articles, were in favor of free trade, by which they could buy their merchandise in the cheapest market, whether it was foreign or domestic.

Though I do not hope to reconcile a discordance of views founded on a diversity of private interests, I shall endeavor to state with fairness the principal arguments by the parties severally supporting their respective tenets.

The friends of manufactures, which they too exclusively regard as domestic industry, maintain that it is our true policy to manufacture for ourselves those articles of which our country at once produces the raw materials and possesses the requisite labor and capital; and although, by the greater cheapness of human labor in some foreign countries, where the laborer is obliged to put up with the bare necessaries of life, together with the greater cheapness of capital in such countries, they may be able to undersell our manufacturers, that we are bound, by taxing the foreign articles, to protect the industry of our own citizens from the rivalship of foreign paupers, who are as much below them in the modes of subsistence as in their political condition; and farther, that the higher price which may be paid for the domestic manufacture is but temporary; since the competition among the domestic manufacturers when the home market has been secured to them, together with the gradual increase of skill and of capital, will make the domestic fabrics cheaper and cheaper, until they will eventually be able to support themselves without public protection against foreign competitors. The success of the manufactures of cotton are relied on to prove the soundness of this policy; and it is urged that a similar course pursued towards the manufactures of iron, wool, leather, and some other articles, would be attended with similar results; and lastly, that even if the domestic manufacture should not always become cheaper than it could be purchased abroad, the difference would be more than compensated by securing a supply, from domestic sources, of all articles essential to the comfort of our citizens, rather than to be dependent on the good-will, the peace, and the varying productiveness of other nations.

Their opponents, on the other hand, insist that the manufactures purchased by the exchanges of commerce are as much the product of domestic industry as if they were fabricated at home; since they have been obtained only by being given in exchange for commodities which are the product of our own land and labor; and that it is one of the highest boasts of political freedom that every citizen should have an unrestricted right to buy where he can obtain the cheapest and best articles, or those which he thinks the cheapest and best; and to compel him, by a tax on the cheaper foreign article, to buy a dearer one made at home, is to take money out of his pocket to put it into the pocket of another, and is therefore an act of tyranny and injustice; that, although the protected manufacture may, perchance, in time become cheaper, this result is problematical, since many articles, after a protection of forty or fifty years, cannot even then dispense with it; and that the loss is present and certain, while the benefit is future and contingent: that if other countries can make cloth, cutlery, or railroad iron cheaper than we, whether they owe their advantage to their pauper labor, their greater skill, or more abundant capital, we should be wise to profit by this cheapness, as we are when we import our pine-apples rather than raise them in hot-houses, and bring our tea from the farthest extremity of the globe rather than raise it at home, as Mr. Junius Smith has shown that we might do.

That, inasmuch as the sagacity of self-interest will commonly induce individuals to employ their capital and industry in the most profitable modes, the policy which induces many to abandon their previous pursuits to engage in manufacturing may be presumed to divert labor and capital to a business less suited to the circumstances of the country, and is so far a source of national loss.

That, from the great distance of foreign manufacturers from our country, the cost of transporting their fabrics hither — comprehending freight, insurance, commissions, and interest of money — is a standing bounty and encouragement to domestic manufacturers, which are likely to prompt the establishment of all those that are adapted to the circumstances of the country; and when they are further stimulated by an impost, rash and improvident enterprises, ruinous to the undertakers and injurious to the nation, are often the consequence.

That, while it is a wise policy for a country to secure a domestic supply of everything essential to the national defence, all further interference by the government is injurious. That a dependence on foreign countries for any commodities it may require has advanced the cause of civilization in the world, and been of more benefit than disadvantage to its separate communities.

Amidst this discrepancy of views, I think it will be admitted by the advocate of free trade that where the country possessing the raw materials, skill, and capital required for a manufacture, is so far ripe for it that a temporary encouragement will enable it to overcome the early difficulties which attend on every new business, and finally to support itself, such encouragement may be justified, and the country be more than compensated by the new manufacture for the previous cost of protection.

But, on the other hand, without this result, the advocate for protective restrictions must admit that they not only take money from one class of men to give to another, but also take a further sum, which is given to no one, and is, in fact, so much value annihilated. Thus, suppose that a ton of bar-iron could be imported and sold, free of duty, for $60, and that iron of a similar quality could not be made here and sold for less than $75 a ton, and that the profit to the iron-master is $10 a ton. Now, let us suppose that, to secure the home market to the domestic producer, an impost of $20 the ton is laid on this iron. The purchaser, then, of a ton, in giving $75, gives $15 more than the foreign iron would cost; of which $10 is merely transferred from him to the iron-master, but $5 is received by no one, and is as thoroughly destroyed as if it had been sunk in the ocean.

CHAPTER XI.

MENTAL INDUSTRY.

In treating of profitable industry, we must not pretermit mental labor, which contributes so largely to all the higher interests of the State. Intellectual industry may be classed under the higher public functionaries: the three professions of law, physic, and divinity; instructors of youth; cultivators of practical science, such as engineers, chemists, astronomical observers; and authors. Though the public functionaries all receive pecuniary compensation, yet a considerable part of their remuneration consists in the honor conferred by the office, it being an evidence of merit in the officer, and of the favor of those who appointed him.

The profession of the law, in countries where the knowledge of civil and political rights is much cultivated, especially fits men for public employments. Accordingly, a very large majority of the higher civil functionaries, both in the General and State Governments, have been taken from this profession. The judges, a corps of great power and influence, can be taken from no other. Of the fifteen Presidents of the United States, all but General Washington, General Taylor, and Mr. Madison (who was educated for the bar), had been practising lawyers.

A consequence of this success of the legal profession

is, that the honors and emoluments obtained by it constitute a part of its recommendation, and swell the list of its competitors, so as to reduce the average remuneration received by this class to the level of that received by other classes, in proportion to the intellectual and moral qualities which they put in requisition. These, however, it must be remembered, are very high. To be an eminent and successful lawyer requires the gift of unwonted powers of speech, either for reasoning or persuasion, and the moral qualities of integrity and discretion. He must be faithful, not only to the interests, but often also to the secrets of his client; and he must be superior to the temptation of taking advantage of that client's necessities or difficulties. These species of moral worth they rarely fail to possess; and, in the higher departments of the profession, no class of men have a more exalted sense of honor, or the obligations of conscience.

In the practice of medicine, high intellectual and moral qualities are also required, and are also frequently found; but, as the merits of a practitioner in this profession cannot be brought to the same ready and easy test as those of a clergyman or lawyer, there is in it a greater number of unworthy pretenders, who profit by the general desire of health or relief from disease, as well as by the credulity of ignorance, to vend quack medicines, sometimes merely worthless, and sometimes injurious, from which they occasionally derive great gains, as are indicated by the liberal sums paid for advertising their remedies, and by the large fortunes they are known to amass. The secret of a celebrated *panacea* was obtained from a German soldier, in discharge of a debt of twenty dollars, and remained for several years unused by its possessor; but when at length put into operation, and managed with great industry and address, it proved the means of acquiring a fortune of near, or quite, half a million of dollars.

Of the different branches of the healing art, surgery commonly receives the highest rewards, partly on account of the unequivocal relief from great suffering which it often affords, and partly because there is but a small proportion of the medical profession who possess at once the knowledge, the self-command, and the practical skill required in surgery.

Nearly akin to this art, but of an humbler character, is that of the dentist, which, though comparatively of recent origin,* may be regarded as among the most useful of human arts. It is favorable to health by assisting mastication; it aids men in the noble office of speech; and it contributes to make them more agreeable to others. Its followers have, therefore, in half a century, been multiplied more than fifty fold, and most of them receive a very liberal compensation.

---

* I can remember when there was but one dentist in the State of Virginia. He was a German, and his original occupation was that of a farrier.

In the clerical profession, as has been mentioned, a part of the remuneration, besides the gratification of the religious instinct, being the high respect in which it is held, the pecuniary compensation is thereby greatly diminished. The rewards, however, of this description, are often very liberal, and are in proportion to the intellectual and moral qualities, and especially oratorical talents which its followers possess.

The scientific class, comprehending instructors of youth, engineers, and practical chemists and metallurgists, are variously remunerated. The humblest description of teachers commonly obtain a very moderate compensation, partly by reason of the comparative ease of the employment. The irksomeness of bodily labor to those not accustomed to it, will commonly induce a young man to prefer two hundred dollars for keeping a school, to three hundred dollars for cutting down trees or ploughing. Besides, the former occupation has more dignity from its intellectual character. This fact, by recommending the business of teaching, tends to lessen its pecuniary rewards; while, on the other hand, its demand for qualifications above the average required for common laborers, tends to raise them.

Professorships in universities and colleges, requiring both intellectual accomplishments and elevation of moral character, are generally well remunerated. But as their incomes are certain, they are less than those of successful practitioners of law or medicine.

Civil engineers, being employed in the construction of public works of great cost and of national importance, commonly receive a remuneration in proportion to their responsibility. It can easily happen that a difference in the science and sound judgment of two engineers may, in such costly and often difficult enterprises, be equal to one or more hundred thousand dollars. Those, then, who are at the head of the profession, generally obtain very high rewards for their services. Labor of this rank, in fact, is at a monopoly price.

It has been remarked that the inventors of valuable discoveries are commonly ill rewarded, and that the price which the public pays for the new benefit is obtained by a very inferior class of men, who make these discoveries practically useful. The fact is undoubtedly as has been supposed, and the explanation is not difficult.

In the first place, it must be remembered that the reward which the inventive class chiefly regard is fame and the esteem of their fellow-men, which advantages an inventor can best obtain by publishing his discoveries to the world, and thus leaving them to the free use of all competitors. When Jenner discovered the preventive virtue of the cow-pox, he might probably have derived large gains by keeping the secret to himself. So of Watt's steam-engine; and the use of ether and chloroform in relieving pain.

But, secondly, even if the man of science were desirous of rendering his discoveries a source of pecuniary profit, he is likely to want the requisite qualifications. To embody what he has discovered in fit, visible, and tangible forms, when necessary; to recommend them successfully to the notice and confidence of the public; and to defeat the cavils and hostility which they are certain to encounter, requires a knowledge of men and things, and a talent for business in which the devotees of science are almost always grossly deficient. These business talents are possessed by men very differently trained, who thus benefit themselves by benefiting the public.

In the third place, the want of capital is alone sufficient to render some discoveries and inventions that are pregnant with utility, valueless to their authors. Had Oliver Evans possessed the requisite funds, or the credit to obtain them, it appears incontestable from the little book published by him, that he would have perfected his steam-carriage for ordinary roads; iron tracks would naturally have succeeded, and thus railways would have been anticipated. What he had not the means of effecting, he distinctly and emphatically predicted would soon be accomplished by others.

But of all intellectual labors, those of authors are, in general, the worst rewarded. Now and then, indeed, a popular writer receives a liberal remuneration; but, for one of this description, there are probably fifty failures, and perhaps twenty who do not receive for their efforts in this way the pay of a common laborer.

A main cause of this signal want of success seems to be the large number of competitors for the public favor, of this class, arising from the very lively desire of literary distinction, and the self-delusion which inspires the hope of attaining it; so that a great majority of the books published meet with the neglect and oblivion which they justly merit.

A small number of authors, having at once rare merit and good fortune, are very highly remunerated, for they are able to command monopoly prices. Those of average merit, who are best rewarded, are writers of approved school-books, voyages and travels, and, above all, works of fiction. Men pay more freely and liberally for pleasure than instruction; and there are probably an hundred readers of an interesting romance for one of an eloquent sermon.

As a general rule, the remuneration of every species of labor which administers to our pleasures will be certain and liberal. This is strikingly manifested in all the imitative arts, in music, dramatic exhibitions, public shows, and games. In the nobler species—painting and sculpture—we see the elements of high price in the great *demand*, caused by the exquisite pleasure they give; and in the small *supply*, caused by the rarity of the talent exhibited by a first-rate artist. Accordingly a portrait by an eminent painter may sell for five hundred dollars, and a statue by

Canova or Thorwaldsen for from five to ten thousand dollars.* It is not unusual for a great singer or actor to earn several hundred dollars in a week; and the celebrated Jenny Lind, whose tickets of admission were sold at unprecedented prices, is supposed to have earned, in the United States, for herself and her employer, in a single year, more than three hundred thousand dollars. Were Garrick, or Mrs. Siddons, or Talma, now living, and disposed to make the most of their rare gifts, they might probably earn as much.

The compensation which should be received by the public functionaries, particularly by legislators, has been often discussed, and it is a problem of some nicety to decide what rate of pay is most conducive to the public welfare. A very high or very low remuneration has each its respective disadvantages. If it be very low, or, as in the British Parliament, nothing at all, it would confine the office to rich men, or the dependants on rich men, and exclude many who may be superior both in ability and love of country, but who could not afford to give their time gratuitously to the public. In monarchial governments, those who confer their services may be compensated by lucrative places; but in popular governments that would be impracticable, and would be liable, moreover, to the objection of making the legislator dependent on the donor of his profitable

* Powers' Greek Slave has recently sold at auction in England for nine thousand dollars.

office. If, on the other hand, the remuneration be very high, the post is set up as a prize, to be scrambled for by such of the mercenary, the cunning, and the unprincipled as assume the character of being the friends of the people. There is always some danger in making public offices very desirable. The power of appointment, whether exercised by one, a few, or the people at large, is ever exposed to the chance of mistake or abuse. No one of these can certainly distinguish between their flatterers and friends. It is better, therefore, that public men should be the unbiassed choice of the constituent class, than that candidates should offer themselves to be approved or rejected by the people. In this way alone, modest merit, — often the highest merit, — which would shrink from what might seem an ostentatious self-display, would be brought forth from its retirement to high station. It was in this way that the American people procured the invaluable services of George Washington, who never was a candidate for any one of the high offices which he filled; and some of the most meritorious of his successors were almost equally passive in obtaining their elevation.

Upon the whole, it would seem to be most consonant to republican principles that legislators should be paid for their services; that their pay should be such as to enable men of small property to serve, so that the people should be less circumscribed in their choice; but that it should not be so large as to encourage intrigue or corruption, or to give an undue stimulus to mercenary men to obtain it; that the pay should be in proportion to the length of the service — that is, a daily pay rather than an annual salary; and lastly, that the pay which the alteration of the value of money, or any other cause, might make it expedient to change, should never be received by the legislators who made it, but only by their successors. Experience amply justifies those who opposed this part of the Federal Constitution, who objected that, if the members could raise their own compensation, it would expose them to the temptation of paying themselves too liberally, and, at all events, to the suspicions of the people; which, by lessening mutual confidence, is always injurious both to the party suspecting and the party suspected. It is a matter of equal surprise and regret to the friend of popular government, that when Congress, in 1818, gave to its members an annual salary of $1500, the people, disapproving both the mode of pay and its amount, indignantly turned out almost every man who had voted for it; yet when, after the lapse of forty years, the same body gave to its members a salary of double the amount, it has escaped open popular censure. No satisfactory solution has been given of the striking inconsistency.

There are several commodities of great utility and extensive consumption which seem to have equal claims to be regarded as raw produce, and as the product of manufacturing industry. Of this character is sugar, whether made from the cane, the beet, or the maple. So of every kind of wine, of cider, butter and cheese, and vegetable oils.

We have now gone through the subject of labor; yet before we take leave of it, let us pause awhile to notice its great and diversified agency in creating national wealth. Though labor must have the aid of natural agents, yet they would be of little avail without the concurrence of human industry. This so acts upon land as to make it produce the materials of man's aliment twenty-fold, or even fifty-fold of what would be its spontaneous yield. It furnishes him with apparel, derived partly from the animal and partly from the vegetable world, suitable to every season. It enables him to provide commodious dwellings, to afford him warmth in the winter and shade in the summer; to make tools and utensils, in infinite variety, to facilitate his labors, and to enlarge his powers over brute matter. After thus contributing to his more important wants, it augments and multiplies his pleasures. It gives to his edifices and his furniture those forms that are most grateful to his eye or his taste. It ransacks the three kingdoms of nature, both on the land and in the ocean, for materials of aliment, and combines them in endless variety, to make them at once pleasant and wholesome. It ministers to the gratification of all the five senses, and delights his taste and imagination by the cultivation of literature and the fine arts. It exercises the noble faculty of reason to discover and understand the laws both of matter and of mind, and to discharge the various functions of government. Man is, indeed, urged to almost unceasing efforts to win the means of subsistence; but he is amply rewarded for his toils by the result of those very efforts, and is always rising in dignity by obeying the instinctive desire of promoting his own happiness.

Every faculty of the mind, whether it be intellect or sense, is thus put in requisition, and they all contribute — each in its way — to the complicated machine of civil society. The powers of man over matter are ever enlarging, either in overcoming its diversified forms of resistance, or in making it subservient to some purpose of utility, greater or less, from a lucifer-match, or daguerreotype, to a railroad or steamship; and thus it may be said, without a metaphor, that, by the exercise of the endowments with which he has been so liberally gifted, he is the artificer of his own condition.

CHAPTER XI.

CAPITAL.

We will now consider the third great source of national wealth — capital; by which is meant that portion of the former products which has been saved for future use, and which may consist of provisions, of raw materials, of manufactured goods, or of money, which is exchangeable for them all.

Capital contributes to production in three ways. *First.* It is indispensable to the execution of any useful or profitable operation; since, unless the materials for the work, and provisions to feed the workmen, or their equivalent, had been previously saved by some one, the operation could not be performed. Without this preliminary saving, man would be unable to build, forge, weave, mine, plow, sow, or reap; nor could he engage in commerce without the previous accumulation of capital.

Secondly. Capital is productive by being converted into labor-saving machines. In this way it may produce many times the value expended. Thus, to take one of the simplest forms of such machinery — a wheelbarrow. By means of the capital laid out in making this machine, a man may transport in a day three or four times as much as he could carry on his shoulders. The profits of a cart or wagon, as the means of transport, would be yet more considerable. To give another example, suppose two men to want a large quantity of plank for building. Instead of sawing it by their own hands, at the rate of from one to two hundred feet in a day, they might, by employing themselves a few weeks in erecting a saw-mill, turned by running water, obtain more plank in a month, and with far greater ease, than they could by their whip-saw in a year. Man can also, by means of tools, which his previous savings have enabled him to provide, often achieve a mastery over brute matter to which his unaided natural powers would be utterly inadequate. Without a saw, for example, or other tool, he would have been incapable of making a plank by his personal efforts.

Thirdly. Capital is productive by enabling its possessor to have the benefit of co-operation, or what has been called "the division of labor;" which often, as we have seen, so greatly increases production. Without capital, a manufacture, the different parts of which may be advantageously distributed among several workmen, cannot be carried on; but with it, the power of production may be prodigiously multiplied, and the cost of the article produced be proportionally cheapened.

By the first of these three modes, capital merely changes its form, without adding to the exchangeable values in the community; but by the two last, the quantity of useful products having been greatly augmented, the effect is partly to make those products cheaper, and partly to add to the exchangeable values or the capital of the community. Thus, suppose a certain amount of capital vested in a manufactory of nails. The consumers of those articles will be gainers by their greater cheapness, and the whole community will have gained by the amount thus saved, and by the profit accruing to the manufacturer after repaying the cost of the raw material and labor expended.

Capital is of two kinds—circulating and fixed. By circulating capital is meant that portion which, having been vested in raw materials or labor, is consumed and reproduced in some manufacture or profitable operation. Of this character are the wool or cotton worked up, and the pay of the workmen in manufacturing those articles. So the iron and labor expended in the fabrication of hardware or cutlery; and the capital thus consumed is reproduced, and again circulates in the manufactured article. It yields a profit only by circulation. Fixed capital consists of those articles employed in any productive operation, which are not thereby consumed, but may be repeatedly used, until they are worn out; such as the buildings, machinery, and tools of a manufactory. The fixed capital of a tailor is his shears, his goose, and his shop, if it belong to him. If he merely rents it, then the rent, like the cloth he works up, is a part of his circulating capital. Fixed capital yields profit without exchanging hands.

Capital, like land and labor, has its appropriate remuneration. What are called the profits of capital, both popularly and by some political economists, means the entire gains of any extensive employment of capital; but where the profit has been the fruit of the personal superintendence and judicious management of the owner, that is properly the wages of labor, and the residue is alone the profits of capital, which is the same thing as the interest of money.

Interest, or a compensation for the use of money or capital lent, has been in some countries deemed unjustifiable, and therefore prohibited. But this was when money, hoarded away, brought no profit to the lender, and when the borrower, wanting it only to spend, derived no profit from the use of it. Where, then, the lender had sufficient security for the repayment of the loan, it seemed unconscientious to demand also interest.

But after communities became commercial and industrious, and money could be made by the use of money, it was as reasonable that a consideration should be paid for the use of capital, as that rent should be paid for land, or hire for the use of a slave or a horse. Where, by an outlay of capital, a labor-saving machine, yielding large profits, could be procured, it could make no difference whether a rent was paid for the machine, or an interest on the money required for its purchase.

Besides, a present pleasure outweighs one that is distant and future. When, therefore, one forbearing to use the means of present gratification, transfers them to another by way of loan, he has a fair claim, when the money is returned, to a further compensation for the delay, and for his forbearance; or, in other words, interest, which thus rewards privation or abstinence, as rent pays for the use of land, and wages for the toils of labor.

The profits of capital or interest, like everything else exchangeable, obeys the law of supply and demand; and is higher or lower, according to its abundance and the field for its employment. In general, interest is high in newly-settled countries, where the more profitable modes of employing capital have not been pre-occupied; and as a country advances in population and wealth, interest commonly declines. In England, in the 15th century, it was 10 per cent. It then successively fell to 8, 6, and at last to 5 per cent. But the government is able to borrow at about 3½ per cent., and the public securities, at the ordinary price, do not yield more; while in all the new British colonies, whether in Australia, Cape of Good Hope, New Zealand, or North America, interest is high. There is a striking difference in this respect between the new and the old States of the Union — interest being much higher in the first than the last.

But everywhere the market rate of interest is liable to incessant fluctuations, according to the variations in the supply or the demand for capital.

Thus, interest rises when there is a deficiency in the supply of money, as where, from any cause, it has been largely exported. Capital is also scarce, and interest proportionally high, in countries where the exactions of the government prevent the accumulation of capital, both by discouraging industry, and lessening the little it does earn. By reason of this insecurity of capital, interest, both in India and China, is 10 or 12 per cent. per annum. The same effect is produced by an increased demand, whether it be caused by the opening of new branches of trade which promise great profits, or by an unwonted enlargement of the old branches.

Sometimes, again, the augmented demand is caused by the indebtedness of the community, in consequence of previous over-trading. This occurred in New York, and some other States, in 1837, when the market rate of interest was unusually high, though the currency was confessedly more distended than usual. These two facts seemed, to the New York Commissioners of the Safety Fund, inconsistent with the received doctrines of political economy; but the apparent inconsistency was readily explained by the fact, that the increase of debt (in consequence of the very extensive speculations in the public lands,) tended to raise the rate of interest yet higher than the increased currency tended to lower it.

The market rate of interest is also affected both by the amount of the loan, and the time for which it is made. Interest is generally less in loans for large sums than for small ones. The difference is the result of several circumstances. There are many more persons who are both willing and able to borrow a small amount than a large one. The field for safe investment of great capitals is a limited one; and of the greatest, governments are the principal borrowers —private individuals, though they might be willing enough to borrow, not often being able to give the required security. Governments can commonly borrow at an annual interest of 3 or 4 per cent., while individuals pay a much higher rate, according to the amount and the estimated risk.

It is said that there are individuals in London who make a livelihood by lending £10 or £12 to the women who sell oranges, cakes, &c. Five shillings is the sum lent to each one, for a day, for which she pays sixpence, which is at the enormous rate of more than 3000 per cent. in a year.

The effect of the duration of the loan on the rate of interest is not uniform. As a general rule, large loans, where the security is undoubted, are made at a lower rate than small ones. This arises from the known difficulty of lending large sums with satisfactory security, by reason of which the capitalist will take a lower rate of interest rather than be soon compelled to seek a new investment, and to incur a loss of interest by the delay. Thus Congress, when, in 1824, it voted a liberal pecuniary donation to La Fayette, for the purpose of enhancing its value, created a stock for the special purpose, and made it payable at a distant day; in consequence of which, it was sold in the market above par. A similar course, from a similar motive, was pursued by the States of South Carolina and Louisiana, in their donations to the daughter of Mr. Jefferson; and the stock, of which those donations consisted, was sold for 10 per cent. above its par value.

But where the sums lent are of a small or moderate amount, a different rule often prevails, and lenders will take a less interest for a small term than a long one. There are always sums of money, in a wealthy community, which are for a time unemployed, and which the owners are not willing to put long beyond their control. They are therefore willing to lend them for a short time at a low interest, on condition that the money will be returned when demanded, but which they would not lend for a long term, even at a high interest, such as may always be commanded from a portion of the community.

In newly settled fertile countries, like many of these States, the raw products of the soil are abundant and cheap, from the large supply of good land, while the price of labor and the market rate of interest are both high, from the wide field open to both for profitable employment; and the general tendency of both labor and capital is to decline with the increase of numbers. But there is no necessary connection between the two. If, from any cause, capital does not increase with the population, — whether from high taxes, a decline of industry, or a want of frugality, — then interest will remain unchanged, though labor has fallen. Such is the condition of China and Hindostan. On the other hand, the supply of capital may increase faster than that of labor, as it does in England, and, consequently, the market rate of interest may there continue to fall, though the price of labor, from its undiminished field of employment, may be unchanged in value.

While the rent of land and wages of labor are left everywhere to regulate themselves according to the laws of supply and demand, the profits of capital, or interest of money, has been, in almost all countries, regulated by law; which, aiming to protect borrowers from the extortion of the lenders, fixes the highest rate of interest, which lenders are forbidden to exceed, under a penalty. This prohibition has probably arisen partly from the ancient prejudice against taking any interest at all, and partly from the general sympathy of mankind with borrowers and debtors rather than with the lenders. But as these laws interfere with the freedom of individual action, and impose a restraint on the terms of hiring capital, which is manifested toward no other voluntary contracts, they have been vehemently opposed as repugnant both to policy and justice. They, however, still retain their place in most codes; and the questions which still present themselves are, What are the present effects of these usury laws, and what would be the consequences of their repeal?

The usury laws tend in several ways to injure the class which they were designed to serve. In the first place, they lessen the amount of money that is ready to be lent; many persons being unwilling either to violate or evade the law, who therefore seek to employ their capital themselves in some way that promises them the market rate of interest, rather than to lend it at the lower legal rate.

But, secondly, when a lender is willing to incur the risk of violating the law, he will naturally seek to indemnify himself for that risk by requiring a higher rate of interest.

Thirdly, where the law is evaded, as it commonly is, by various roundabout proceedings devised by the combined wit of borrowers and lenders, the borrower is thus subjected to additional trouble, and probable loss, which he might avoid if he could directly contract for a loan. So that, upon the whole, the effect of the law is not so much to abolish usury as to make it more burdensome to the debtor class.

It seems probable that the law is, in another way, injurious to the same class. The sympathy which the generality of mankind have ever shown for debtors, and the odium which has always more or less attended those who were disposed to take advantage of their necessities, are somewhat strengthened by the law; and thus men who are very sensitive as to the opinion of their fellow-citizens are unwilling to obtain a higher rate of interest than the law allows, even when they can do so without incurring its penalties. They might, for instance, buy bonds or promissory notes not yet due at a discount far exceeding the legal interest. This practice, which is very frequent with those who would derive a large profit from their moneyed capital, and which is popularly called *shaving*, though it infringes no law, is just as odious and discreditable as direct usury, which is illegal. The difficulty, then, of obtaining loans is still farther increased by the law.

But what would be the consequences of repealing the usury laws? The repeal would remove restraints on a class of contracts in which legislative interposition seems to be no more required than in any other, and so far it would tend to make the laws consistent and uniform. It would also take away the inducement which now exists for one who has borrowed money at usurious interest to act dishonorably, by violating his own solemn engagements. But it is a mistake to suppose that it would greatly increase the loanable money of the community. In a very large majority of the cases of money lent at more than legal interest, the parties resort to the ready expedients of evading the usury law, which merely causes them some little delay and trouble, as by the sale of stock or merchandise to the borrower, on a credit, which is then sold by him at a reduced price for cash; or by the borrower's giving his bond to a friend, who then sells it to the money-lender at a discount for cash. These expedients, and many others for escaping the penalties of usury, are strictly legal, and could not be prohibited without too much restricting commercial intercourse.

The principal effect, then, of the repeal would be to make such evasive shifts and contrivances unnecessary, and to allow a more simple and direct course of procedure between the borrower and lender, without a sensible increase in the amount of money to be lent, or in the facility of borrowing. Hence it is that whenever the experiment of repealing the usury laws has been made, as has been done in several of the States, the public has been disappointed in not seeing the expected benefits, and the repealing law has been itself repealed before its effects had been fairly tested. It is not improbable, too, that such repeals have been furthered by some cases of exorbitant usury, which, being then first openly made, shocked men's natural sense of justice; though similar contracts may have always existed, but having been negotiated in secret, were known only to the parties; and, it might be that such cases of extreme improvidence in one party, and extreme unconscientiousness in the other, might have been made on more reasonable terms, if the parties had waited until the increased competition among the class of lenders had adapted the money market to the new state of things. It may, therefore, be wise in legislatures, in repealing the usury law, to postpone the operation of their act, that the community may prepare for the change.

The injustice which the usury laws do to the moneyed class is greatly mitigated by means of banks, insurance companies, and other joint-stock associations, the price of whose stock, compared with their ordinary dividends, denotes the market rate of interest with tolerable correctness. Thus, suppose the price of a share of stock to be $80, and the ordinary dividend to be $6 per annum; the purchaser of stock would then receive 7½ per cent. for his purchase-money. Those persons who have unemployed funds, but cannot use them in any profitable employment which requires personal attention, by reason of their age, sex, or engrossing occupations, can thus, without labor or care, obtain the current rate of interest by the purchase of stock.

Besides the variations in the rate of interest, according to the amount lent, and the duration of the loan, there is also a difference arising from the character of the employment. When that is low and disreputable, its profits, like the wages of labor, must be proportionally higher. But the chief cause of the difference in the rate of profit is the difference of risk. Thus, capital vested in mining, insurance companies, and in untried enterprises, will require a return much larger than is yielded by government stocks, the profits of which are not precarious. The like uncertainty, but to a less extent, is to be found in the stocks of banks and railroads. But the power which banks possess of accommodating their stockholders with large loans, when the use of money is unusually profitable or desirable, tends to enhance the value of their stock; and that of railroads consists not merely in their dividends, but also in the effect on the value of the neighboring lands. This alone is often a sufficient compensation to many of the stockholders.

It sometimes has been asked, what is the minimum rate to which the interest of money can fall? It is clear that capital cannot increase in a country, unless the whole amount annually produced exceeds the amount annually consumed, and this excess must result from the disposition of individuals to save being greater than their disposition to spend. It seems fair to presume that the disposition to save will diminish with the decline of interest, since the desire of spending for present gratification, which would be overcome by one rate of profit, might not yield to an inferior profit, and thus a further saving might be arrested.

There are, indeed, individuals of such settled habits of frugality and aversion to expense, that they would rather save than spend, though they were to receive no additional profit whatever from their savings. But with a majority of the community, the money saved by them is profitably invested, and the prospect of this profit has been a strong incentive to their economy. Let this hope of profit be taken away, or be greatly diminished, and the desire of further accumulation might be countervailed by the pleasure of spending as well as the relaxation of industry, until the whole amount consumed might equal the amount produced, when, of course, interest would be stationary.

At what rate of interest this resting-point would be reached, is a question which has yet to be determined; but it seems probable that, if interest should ever become so low as one per cent., or even be much under two per cent., further accumulation would then be arrested.

There are circumstances which tend to retard this result, and may even prevent it. Whenever interest becomes very low in any country, capital will naturally find a vent in other nations, connected with it by commercial intercourse, in which it is less abundant. English capital is thus found in every part of the United States, from the Atlantic cities to the remotest regions of the West; and interest might long ago have reached its minimum in Holland, if its capital had not found employment in other countries.

We will now proceed to consider that portion of the capital of a country which consists of its money.

CHAPTER XII.

MONEY.

THE money of a community performs very important functions, and has laws and principles of its own. It is characterized by a degree of mobility or activity to which no other species of capital can approach. There are few commodities which change hands more than once or twice in passing from the producers to the consumers, where they disappear and terminate; but a piece of money or coin may be passing from hand to hand from the time it is struck off at the mint until it is worn out; during which course of circulation, it may have been received and paid away by thousands, and traversed more miles of space than would encircle the globe. In treating of this important agent in all civilized countries, we will successively consider its origin, its functions, and its laws.

1. As to its origin. Though it renders most essential services to society, especially in saving time and labor, it must not be supposed, as has sometimes been done, that a perception of these benefits has led to its adoption. This is no more the case than that the advantages of literature caused the invention of letters. In the progress of society, mankind are

gradually led, by their instinctive wants and desires, to the discovery and adoption of what will afford gratification to those wants and desires; and they thus occasionally light on contrivances and expedients which prove to possess a degree of utility that had never been foreseen.

The process by which money, or a common medium of exchange, was first introduced, seems to have been as follows: At first, the diversified wants of individuals would lead them to exchange some article that they possessed for another which was more desirable to them; and by such exchange each party was benefited, or received more value than he parted with. Hence the practice of barter, which we find to exist in the rudest stages of society. But its advantages are, in the nature of things, very circumscribed. One man, wishing to exchange cloth for bread, may not meet with one who possessed bread and wanted cloth; another, owning a horse, might wish to exchange him for several articles which no single individual was likely to possess, and the horse could not be parcelled out among all those who had the articles he wanted. These, and the like difficulties, in the practice of barter, would naturally induce men, when they could not by exchange obtain the precise article they wanted, to seek that commodity which was in most general request, and which could be kept without loss or deterioration. In this way, by degrees, some species of property would become more generally desired, until it became a common medium of exchange, or money. Thus, in pastoral nations—the first in which men began to accumulate property—cattle and sheep became a currency; and money is thought to have borrowed its name,* in some languages, from this circumstance. These animals, being fed by natural pastures, could be kept not only without loss, but with positive gain, arising from their growth and their multiplication, as well as their milk. When Kentucky was first settled, and steam had not yet facilitated the navigation of the Mississippi, cattle, horses, and hogs afforded the only means of traffic with the Atlantic region. They were accordingly received by the country merchant in exchange for his goods; and when he had become possessed of enough to make a drove, they were transported on foot to the Atlantic States with more celerity and at a less expense than any other species of property. Other commodities have in like manner grown up to be the currency in other countries, as the grains of cocoa in Mexico, salt and slaves in Africa, etc.

But no articles whatever have so generally recommended themselves to the adoption of mankind for the purpose of money as silver and gold; and we find evidence in the Bible that thousands of years ago those metals were the common measures of value and the general mediums of exchange.

---

* As in *pecunia*, from *pecus*.

We see the source of this superiority in the qualities they possess. In the first place, it was important that they should have intrinsic value in the eyes of mankind, and this they possess in their brilliancy and beauty — they being by all classes of men, whether rude or civilized, prized as personal ornaments. Their unequalled lustre gives an excitement and gratification to the sense of vision that is given by nothing else except the precious stones, which, for the same reason, have always been highly valued by mankind. Besides this fundamental quality of being desirable for their own sake, their exchangeable value was increased by their scarcity, and the labor of procuring them. Nature has been very profuse in her production of iron, lead, and copper, but very sparing in that of gold and silver; and to their consequent extraordinary value in the market they owe their portability, by which they can be transmitted to a great distance at little comparative cost, and serve to defray the expenses of travel in remote countries.

Another advantage of these metals is their uniformity. One piece of gold, wherever found, has the same specific gravity, the same malleability and ductility, and nearly the same color, as every other piece. So as to silver. They are also capable of being divided into small portions, to suit different degrees of value; and those portions can be at pleasure reunited into a homogeneous mass by melting. Another recommendation of these metals is that they are not liable to change, especially gold; most other metals being more or less acted on by air or water, so as to oxidate or rust. There are numerous coins in the collections of the curious which were struck two thousand years ago, and are apparently unchanged. And lastly, they are capable of receiving an impression, by being moulded or stamped, so that they can be readily identified, and their exchangeable value known by inspection.

The utility of these metals for ornament is greatly augmented by their being malleable into leaves of extreme thinness, so that with a small portion a great surface can be covered over. An ounce of gold, when beaten into leaf, would gild 166 square feet of surface. In like manner, it may be drawn into wire so small as to be scarcely discernible to the naked eye.

By reason of these recommendations, gold and silver are used for money in every quarter of the world; and one or both are made the standard of the value of everything else.

In countries in which those metals are neither produced nor can be obtained by commerce in sufficient abundance, various substitutes for a currency have been resorted to. Thus, in the early settlement of the British colonies on this continent, where gold and silver were scarce, substitutes were found in commodities which were extensively used in commerce. Tobacco was thus used in Virginia and

Maryland, fish in New England, rice in South Carolina, and in most of those colonies a paper currency, consisting of written engagements by the colonial governments to pay money, which were receivable for all dues at the public treasury.

2. The useful functions of money are very great in all civilized countries. It can be accommodated to all exchanges, whether of small or large amount; and it thus saves the time and labor which would be required by the circuitous, tedious, and imperfect process of barter. It encourages productive industry, by enabling a manufacturer, by a single exchange, or set of exchanges, to dispose of his fabrics in large quantities; and as some have money, which, from their age, their sex, or their other occupations, they cannot personally manage, while there are others who possess the enterprise and capacity for employing it profitably, it can be transferred from one to the other, to the advantage of both parties.

Money also gives great facilities to governments in the collection of their revenue, which would be otherwise collected in bulky articles; transported at a great expense, and be liable to waste, injury, and peculation. There would be the same advantage in disbursing the revenue as in collecting it; and lastly, it enables one country to pay its debts to another, in their commercial intercourse, by a commodity of universal circulation, which can be transported with more safety, and at less expense, than any other.

The useful offices of money are indeed so great and so various, that it would seem impossible for a community to execute the complicated and diversified purposes of civilized life without such a general medium of exchange.

Though the functions of money are of such importance, yet, as its materials are very costly, it is desirable to have as little of it as will suffice to perform its useful purposes. To have twice as much money in a community as its circumstances require, is as unwise as to have an hundred wagons for transport when fifty would be sufficient; or two bridges to cross a stream at the same place.

The quantity of money required in a country depends partly on the value of the money, and partly on the number and amount of its ordinary exchanges.

The value of the precious metals, like that of other products of human industry, depends on the cost of procuring them; and, from their natural scarcity, their value has been always very high, in proportion to their bulk, and that value is uniform at the same time and place. But it varies very greatly in different ages and in different countries. Thus, it has generally been considered that the discovery of America, by reason of the unwonted richness of its mines, lowered the value of those metals from one-third to one-fourth of their previous value; and the recent discoveries of gold in California and Australia seem destined to lower the value of that metal — to what extent will be hereafter considered.

These metals have also very different values in different places. The principal cause of this diversity is the difference of distance from the most productive mines — the value increasing with the distance. They are thus dearer in Europe than America, and in Asia than in Europe.

It might seem at first that, when a commodity contains so much value in a small bulk and weight as gold, its transportation would be proportionally cheap, and that the cost of carriage could not add much to its value. Thus, 100 pounds of gold would be worth about $20,000, the freight of which, 3000 miles by water, would not be more than $2, and by railroad about thrice as much. The insurance and other charges would scarcely exceed the half of one per cent. Let us, however, suppose the whole expense of transport to be $200. This would be but one per cent. of the value of the gold, which seems to indicate that such value must be nearly the same at a distance of 3000 miles from the mines as at the mines themselves. But it must be recollected that the gold, thus transmitted to a distant country, must be purchased by the products of that country; and that these being probably of great bulk compared with their value, the cost of their transport is proportionally high; and that the payment of this expense is an indispensable prerequisite to the transfer of the gold from the mines. It must, therefore, be added to the cost of the gold in the distant country. Besides, if the mining country produces little else for foreign exchange than gold, as is sometimes the case, then the cost of the gold transported must be enhanced by the expense of two voyages.

Another circumstance which influences the quantity of these metals in each country is its wealth. Rich countries having more exchanges to make, and to a larger amount, require more gold and silver than poor ones.

The substitution of paper money for specie, and other expedients for economising the use of the precious metals, has a tendency to diminish their amount. This circumstance in England may tend as much to lessen its specie currency as its great wealth tends to increase it.

The combined influence of all these circumstances is shown in the amount of gold and silver required by each country in proportion to its population. In Great Britain, the amount to each inhabitant is about $16. In France, where bank paper is much less used, but where there has not been as great an accumulation of wealth as in England, it is $12. In the other parts of Europe, it is much less. In the United States, supposing their present population to be thirty millions, it is about $8. It is much reduced by the very extensive use of bank paper.

The quantity of money wanted in a country, being

in proportion to the amount of its exchanges, is affected by various circumstances. Thus, where land is a common subject of traffic, as it is in most parts of the United States, more money is required on that account than in countries where it seldom changes hands, as in most parts of Europe. In slaveholding countries, too, so large an addition to the exchangéable property requires an addition to their currency. This circumstance adds to the money required in the Southern States, but it is probably more than counterbalanced by the general practice of the agricultural class in dealing with their merchants on credit, and settling their accounts but once a year. It is not uncommon there for men whose annual expenses are from two to three thousand dollars, but who rarely have by them more than an hundred dollars in specie.

In the fluctuations to which the circulating money of a country is subject, it sometimes has an excess beyond what the exchanges of the community actually require, and sometimes a deficiency, both of which have their inconveniences. When there is a redundancy of money, its value naturally falls, and the prices of other commodities rise, which is injurious to the foreign trade. It is also detrimental to the class of creditors, and advantageous to the debtors. It does mischief, too, by presenting the delusive appearance of a rise in the value of property, which sometimes leads to an increased expenditure, and, what is worse, engenders a spirit of speculation. The natural corrective of the evil is the export of the excess of specie to foreign countries.

The deficiency of circulating medium produces for the time more sensible mischief. It checks all useful enterprise, and often suspends the operations of productive industry. The manufacturer, not meeting with the customary vents for his fabrics, is obliged to discharge his workmen, and to stop his purchases of raw materials. The wheels of commerce all move slowly and heavily, or stop altogether. Imports are discouraged, and it is only by the stimulus which low prices give to the export trade that this evil can be remedied by the import of specie. It greatly impedes, and sometimes totally arrests, the collection of debts, by making their pressure so much more heavy; and it is thus an evil both to debtors and creditors.

This evil is commonly, in the United States, the consequence of too heavy importations of foreign goods; which, when not attended or closely followed by an adequate amount of exports, the deficiency is paid in specie, which, being principally drawn from the banks, compels them either to suspend cash payments or to call in much of what they had previously lent; thus, in either case, occasioning embarrassments and difficulties that are felt by all classes.

It is not, however, correct to suppose, as has been done by those who reason in political economy as if it were a mathematical instead of a moral science, that the value of the circulating specie rises or falls in full proportion to its excess or deficiency. Thus, suppose the amount of such specie to be suddenly doubled, its value would not therefore sink to one-half. By the force of habit, a man would not soon give $200 for a horse, or an acre of land, which had previously sold for $100. A part of the excess would, indeed, be balanced by depreciation; but a part, also, would be inoperative, by reason of a larger amount of idle, unemployed money, and by many purchases being now made for cash which had before been made on credit. Individuals would carry in their pockets, and banks retain in their vaults, specie to a larger amount in value than before.

In like manner, if the circulating specie was reduced to one-half, the consequence would be, not a duplication of its value, but a part of the deficiency would be counterbalanced by an increase of sales on credit instead of for cash, together with a diminution of the deposits in the banks and in the hands of individuals, and the residue in the reduction of nominal prices, and the rise in the value of the precious metals. As to the prices of commodities, there would be, whether in the case of deficiency or of excess, a great difference in different articles. Of those commodities which find their market in foreign countries, the prices at home would be governed by the prices abroad. But the principal effect of the change would be confined to the prices of land and of those domestic products which find their market at home.

The better to fit the precious metals to perform the offices of currency, governments have coined them into pieces adapted to popular use. They have with jealous rigor reserved to themselves the exclusive right of coining, which has ever been regarded as an appropriate and important function of sovereignty.

The following are the principal regulations of the United States mint. It, in the first place, determines the weight, varieties, and relations of the different coins. By way of securing the advantages of the decimal arithmetic in all reckonings of money, every coin is ten times the value of another below it. Thus, an eagle is equal in value to ten dollars, a dollar to ten dimes, a dime to ten cents, and a cent to ten mills. But it has been found, both in this country and in France, that mankind naturally prefer the binary divisions of halves, quarters, eighths, and sixteenths; and, though the monetary system of the United States has been in operation more than seventy years, the people have never adopted the prescribed currency farther than to keep their accounts in dollars and cents,—which, moreover, is not universal,—or been induced to dispense entirely with the use of the eighths and sixteenths of a dollar of the Mexican coinage. The Government has also deemed it expedient to accommodate the popular preference by coining halves and quarters of the dollar.

In all coins of silver or gold, some alloy of base metal is mingled, for two reasons: one is that the wear of the coin is thereby lessened — and the other is, that since those metals are scarcely ever found perfectly pure, the practice saves the necessity of refining them to extreme purity, which would be often an expensive as well as nice operation.

In some countries the cost of coinage is defrayed by the government; while in others, it is paid for by those who bring bullion to the mint to be coined, and the charge is called a *seignorage*. This charge is perfectly proper and just, there being no more reason why the government should render this service gratuitously than any other. It is further recommended by policy as well as justice. When the coinage is gratuitous, the coins being then of no more value than an equal weight of bullion, are as readily melted up by the manufacturer, or exported by the merchant, as the same amount of bullion, and the expense and loss from coinage are thus augmented. But when money is subjected to a seignorage, it being worth more in the country where it was coined than it is abroad, the loss on exporting it tends to prevent its exportation; and even when it is exported, the same circumstance will often occasion it to be returned to the country where it is most valuable.

There is another important diversity among nations as to money. Some make silver, others gold, and others again both metals, standards of value and legal tenders for debts. Without doubt each metal has its peculiar advantages as a currency. Silver is the best for small values, while gold is far more convenient for large payments. But the policy of having two standards of value does, in fact, often deprive a community of one of the two species of currency which it was intended to secure. When both gold and silver are made standards of value and legal tenders for debts, the law must determine their relative values. But the relative values of these metals, like those of all other commodities, is liable to change, and whenever, in these occasional fluctuations, the market value differs from the legal, the undervalued metal is sure of being that kind of specie which is sent abroad, and is also likely to be sent to the melting-pot of the manufacturer, until it disappears from circulation. Besides, when the undervalued metal is neither melted nor exported, it is likely to be either hoarded or to command a premium in the market, either of which supposes it to be not in general circulation.

When the mint was first established in 1791, the law estimated gold at fifteen times the value of silver. This being found to rate gold too high and silver too low, whenever money was to be sent hither, gold was preferred, while silver was preferred for export; the consequence was, an inadequate supply of silver, so that it generally commanded, for large sums, a premium of 5 per cent. Some years afterwards, gold gradually rose in price, so as to be worth more than fifteen times as much as silver, and then it commanded a premium — the eagles first coined readily selling for half a dollar more than their value by law. Congress subsequently raised the price of gold to *sixteen* times the value of silver, but the California mines have reduced its price; and, to replace the silver currency which had been previously banished from circulation by reason of its being valued too low, a new issue has been made of silver, with a degree of alloy sufficient to counterbalance the recent depreciation of gold. It seems to be a mistake to suppose, as the legislature probably did, that it is necessary to make both metals legal tenders to secure the circulation of both. They are so universally prized, that if they were coined into pieces of convenient size, either of them will be readily taken as money, whether made a legal tender or not. This fact has been more than once evinced in the United States, where foreign coins have always had a ready currency, though they have sometimes not been a legal tender, but also in bank notes, which have never been a legal tender in any State, but which constitute the principal currency in all of them. It then is not merely an absurdity in theory to have two standards whose relative values are always liable to change, but a policy that is practically injurious. Besides silver and gold, copper is generally coined for the payment of small sums, since even a silver coin of the value of a cent would be too small for use. In the United States the copper coins have undergone several changes. They now are rated so much beyond the value of the metal, that they yield a considerable profit to the government.

It is a yet more important proposition that the value of these metals is liable to change, when compared with that of other commodities. Whenever they are procured with more ease, and become more abundant, they must obey the universal law, and become proportionally cheaper. The discovery of America, where mines of unprecedented richness were found, was believed to have, in the course of time, lowered gold to one-third of its former price, and silver to one-fourth; and the recent discoveries of gold in Siberia, California, and Australia, have already produced a fall in the value of that metal, and are likely to produce a much greater. Such a fall is very important in its consequences. In all countries in which gold is a legalized currency, its depreciation lessens the real amount of debts, and is so far an injustice to creditors. It virtually reduces the amount of all national debts, and lessens all incomes derived from money, or from that which, like the shares of joint-stock companies, has only a monetary value.

If the whole amount of gold annually produced exceeds the amount annually consumed, it must necessarily decline in value, and it becomes desirable to know the extent of the depreciation.

The quantity of gold now annually drawn from the mines is estimated at two hundred millions of dollars; and, from present appearances, there is no reason to expect that the production will soon diminish. The annual consumption of this metal may be ranged under four principal heads: 1. Coining; 2. Manufactures and the arts; 3. Wear and tear; 4. Losses at sea. We will briefly notice each of them.

1. Coining. The quantity of gold used in this way has of late greatly increased. In consequence of the abundant supply derived from California and Australia, this metal enters more largely into the currency of those countries where the previous circulation had been principally of silver. This has been the case in France, where gold has taken the place of silver to the amount of several hundred millions of dollars. In the United States also, where silver was formerly the principal currency, gold has been extensively substituted, so as to have probably increased it from less than ten millions of dollars to more than two hundred millions.

But coinage will not add to the present consumption of gold beyond what will be required to meet the increase of traffic consequent on the increase of population and wealth. The whole amount of gold currency in the civilized world is estimated at about fifteen hundred millions of dollars; and supposing the annual increase of wealth to be five or six per cent. a year, — a very liberal estimate, — the yearly addition to the gold currency cannot exceed ninety millions.

2. The consumption in manufactures and the arts. Gold is used so extensively in the manufacture of watch-cases, jewelry, trinkets, and in gilding, that it is not easy to estimate its consumption in this way. In France the annual consumption is computed to be twenty millions of francs — nearly four millions of dollars. Supposing the population of Europe to be eight times that of France, and its consumption of gold to be at half the rate, in proportion to numbers, the whole annual European consumption of gold in this way would be sixteen millions; which, by adding two millions for the consumption of America, would be eighteen millions.

3. The wear and tear of gold in coin, ornaments, and utensils. The whole amount of gold vested in these several ways has been computed at three thousand millions of dollars. The estimated rates of wear and tear vary greatly in different classes of objects. In coins of general circulation, the annual loss has been reckoned at from a four-hundredth to a thousandth part. In some articles of jewelry it may be as much; but in many more it is insignificant. If we suppose it to be a five-hundredth part of the whole amount, the annual consumption from this source would be six millions of dollars.

4. Losses at sea, etc. The amount of these is still more uncertain; but, supposing it to be five millions annually, the total consumption would then be —

For additional coinage..................	$90,000,000
Manufactures and the arts..............	18,000,000
Wear and tear..............................	6,000,000
Losses at sea, etc..........................	5,000,000
Total...........................	$119,000,000

If, then, we estimate the present annual consumption at one hundred and twenty millions, it is little more than half the computed annual production, and a fall in the value of gold must be the inevitable consequence.

But it is not more certain that depreciation will be the consequence of the excess of production over consumption, than that such depreciation would be followed by two effects—a diminution of the supply, and an increase of the demand. First, as to the supply: however the gold may be procured,—whether by washing or mining,—there must be a gradation in the productiveness of the labor and capital employed in obtaining it; and supposing it to decline in value ten or fifteen per cent., then the labor and capital which could not bear that reduction would be thrown out of employment, and the quantity produced be proportionally diminished. And secondly, an increased consumption would as certainly follow in coining and manufactures. Thus, by this twofold effect of depreciation, the supply and the demand of gold—that is, its production and consumption—would finally be equal, and balance each other, when depreciation would cease.

The rate at which the excess of production over consumption would produce depreciation would depend on the proportion which such excess bore to the quantity of coin previously circulating in the commercial world. This quantity, before the discovery of the Californian and Australian mines, was supposed to be about five hundred millions of dollars — now increased to nine hundred millions. If, then, the annual excess of production over consumption is sixty millions, then the annual depreciation ought to be $6\frac{2}{3}$ per cent. But this estimate would be ever liable to be affected by variations in the supply and the demand, so that time alone can give the true and precise solution of the problem.

The consumption or employment of the precious metals for money is greatly diminished by the substitution of paper currency, by which communities have been able to save a large amount of expense, for the purchase of such costly materials as gold and silver; and of all the modes of providing this substitute, none have been found so safe and efficient as the promissory notes of banks — which we will now consider.

CHAPTER XIII.

BANKS.

Of these institutions there are two kinds: banks of deposit, and banks of circulation. Of the first kind, there are but few examples. The most celebrated bank of this description, though not the earliest, was the Bank of Amsterdam, which, in consequence of the inconvenience of the various kinds of foreign money that found their way thither when Holland carried on commerce with all parts of the world, was established to receive these foreign coins on deposit at their fair value; and the receipts for these deposits, issued by the bank, passed from hand to hand as a currency of undoubted credit, and commanded an agio or premium, in lieu of the foreign coins deposited; and, as there was some small deduction or loss in drawing out the money from the bank, it was scarcely ever done. The gold and silver was consequently long steadily increasing, until at length it was found that, after these deposits had been faithfully kept for some centuries, the bank had been tempted to lend out much of this idle treasure to great corporations, to relieve them from pecuniary difficulty, which loans they never found it convenient to repay. The subsequent discovery of these facts destroyed the credit of the bank, and the bank itself. The example has been rarely imitated; and there is, perhaps, no case now existing of a bank of mere deposits.

Banks of circulation, which have been since adopted, are of very great commercial importance, both by their functions and their number.

They are commonly created by a charter from the government, for which they pay a fixed or an annual sum. Being possessed of a large capital, on the credit of this they are enabled to circulate their own promissory notes as a currency. Since their notes are redeemable in gold or silver on demand, they obtain a ready circulation, and are often preferred to specie, from their greater portability, the greater safety and care with which they can be transferred from place to place, and the saving of time in counting large sums.

It is in this substitution of their paper for gold and silver that the bank finds its profit, and the public its advantage; since the banks receive the same interest for their notes as for specie, and the public is a gainer by the substitution of so cheap an article as paper for the precious metals.

Banks of circulation are also banks of deposit—they being the safest depositories of money of all kinds, whether of paper or specie.

They are also banks of discount; that is, they advance the money on the promissory notes of merchants and others not yet due, on *discounting* the interest, and it is chiefly through these borrowers and depositors that their notes get into circulation.

Though their notes are liable to be returned to them to be exchanged for specie as soon as they are issued, yet it is found by experience that by reason of the superior convenience of bank paper over the precious metals in saving time and trouble, a certain proportion of their issues remains some time in circulation. To the extent then which experience justifies, they issue their paper — aiming always to keep as much specie in their vaults as will suffice to meet the ordinary and probable demands for gold and silver; and it is commonly considered that their issues are within the bounds of prudence, if they have not more than three dollars of paper in circulation for one dollar of specie in their vaults. This, however, does not mean three times the amount of their capital stock, even where that stock was altogether in specie, because as soon as the banks begin to lend, a certain portion of the amount lent is specie, in consequence of which they may reach the limit prescribed by prudence (three times as much circulation as specie,) when they had not lent to *double* the amount of their capital.

Whenever, by reason of a sudden panic of distrust with the public, or of heavy drafts of coin for export, the specie of the bank is exhausted, or has become very low, the bank must then go into the market to purchase specie; which, being a recourse likely to affect their credit, they never resort to but in cases of necessity.

When prudently conducted, these institutions are very useful in a commercial community. So far as they make paper supply the place of gold and silver, they enable the country to dispense with a large quantity of those metals; and the capital thus saved may be profitably employed in other branches of domestic industry. By means of cheques or drafts on them, their depositors — comprehending the whole mercantile class, and all men of business — are spared the expense of keeping, counting, and transferring their money; and they greatly diminish the amount of idle specie capital—the little rills of individual depositors swelling the stream in the banks — their means of making loans are thereby augmented. They are more likely than individuals to lend their money to borrowers, who can use what they borrow in a way that will be at once safe to the bank, profitable to themselves, and beneficial to the community — and lastly, they can, by their established credit, give seasonable aid to the government in times of sudden calls for large pecuniary disbursements.

But these benefits are sometimes attended with great drawbacks. Banks are occasionally tempted, with the view of increasing their gains, to enlarge their issues to a point which is consistent neither with their own safety nor the interests of the public.

The consequence of these imprudent issues, whenever the course of trade causes a great export of specie, is probably the failure of the bank to redeem its notes; which immediately checks their circulation, and subjects the people to the evils of a depreciated currency, that embarrasses all the operations of commerce, and deprives creditors of a portion of their debts. Even where this serious result does not take place, the excess of paper is apt to engender a wild spirit of speculation, and to stimulate private extravagance; both of which are sure to be followed by a reaction that is severely felt by the community. Thus, in 1836, when the banks had received a large accession of specie from abroad, in consequence of special orders of the Government, for the purpose of lessening the circulation of bank paper, and increasing that of specie, those institutions, instead of increasing the specie currency, were tempted to distend their loans and issues to an unprecedented amount, so that the sales of the public lands, having then become a favorite object of speculation, were increased from three millions of dollars in a year to twenty millions. The effect of this redundancy of paper money was, in the following year, a general stoppage of the banks, and an extent of private bankruptcy and ruin which had never been witnessed before.

A similar result was witnessed in 1857. In consequence of the large supplies of gold received from California, the banks had all lent liberally, and issued paper in excess. When, then, one of the most unsound of them* became embarrassed, and failed to redeem its notes, a panic with all the rest caused them to suspend cash payments, by which all commercial and manufacturing industry was greatly checked, and, in some cases, entirely arrested.

The first object, therefore, to which these institutions should bend all their efforts, is to keep their issues within the limits of safety. With this view, they are subjected to various restrictions, in addition to those contained in their charters, which are imposed by the stockholders in their by-laws, and sometimes by the president and directors themselves. The most important of these regulations are the following:

In making their loans and discounts, these corporations should not only be guarded as to the amount and the security, but should also attend to the character and purpose of the loans. They should, with rare exceptions, make them for short terms, as sixty or ninety days; the difficulty of foreseeing the vicissitudes of trade being in proportion to the remoteness of the time. They should always prefer discounting that paper which had been given for an actual purchase of merchandise rather than that given merely

* The Bank of Pennsylvania.

to procure money. The former, commonly called "business paper," is the safest, because the maker of the note has received a value equal to the amount of the debt he has contracted with the bank; while the "accommodation paper" may have been an expedient to procure money to spend, or to discharge an old debt, and the bank has not as good an assurance that the borrower will be able to repay his debt when it is due.

There is, indeed, in all the banks, much money lent of the latter description, nor is it always easy or important to avoid it; but many loans of this character are continued for years by a renewal of the notes every term of sixty or ninety days; and it is notorious that, in times of great pressure on the banks, when they aim to get back a portion of what has been thus lent, a curtailment to the amount of ten, or even five per cent., is severely felt by the borrowers.

The issue of small notes, though a source of profit to the banks, is injurious to the public. A dollar note is not more convenient than a gold dollar, and the cost of fabrication may be nearly or quite as much. But the great disadvantage of such notes is that they banish gold and silver from circulation to an equal amount; so that, when, by the course of trade, specie is demanded for exportation, the banks which are first applied to for gold and silver cannot readily obtain from the community what they have paid away. The greater, therefore, the denomination of the smallest notes, the larger is the reservoir from which the banks can supply the specie of which they have been drained, and thus better escape the evils of suspension.

But, more effectually to secure to the public the benefits of banks, and to guard against their mischiefs, the restrictions which the legislature should impose on them seem, principally, to be the following:

No bank should be established without a considerable capital. Sometimes these institutions are brought into existence where they are not wanted, by a few men, to serve their own selfish ends; by some who hope to be salaried officers of the bank; by others, who are needy borrowers; and by others again, who, being eager speculators, are looking forward to the prospect of large loans. It is only when the capital of a bank is large that the public can have a well-founded confidence in its solidity — that its facilities to trade were actually called for, and that its stock is owned by those who, possessing wealth, may be presumed to have the requisite prudence and judgment for its management.

The capital should be scrupulously paid in gold and silver. When a bank goes into operation before its whole capital stock is paid up, as is usual, the money paid on the last instalments is often specie drawn from the bank itself; by which course, its proportion of specie, and consequently both its profits and solidity, are much diminished.

Whenever the banks suspend cash payments, they should always be subjected to some penalty in addition to the loss of their profits. They should be made to pay interest on their notes, when not redeemed, to be recoverable by a short legal process.

Whenever their dividends, or actual profits, exceed a certain prescribed amount, one-half of the excess should be payable into the public treasury. There should be a frequent change of directors, and no one should continue in that office more than a certain number of years.

They should be prohibited from issuing any note under a certain amount. A few of the States have forbidden the issue or circulation of any note under five dollars. An extension of this restraint would be wise. Among many errors in relation to banking and finance into which General Jackson and his advisers were betrayed, there is one piece of policy the wisdom of which even many of his enemies admitted; and this was, that no bank should issue a note of a less denomination than twenty dollars. In that case, there would always be in the community an ample fund on which the banks could draw when pressed for specie.

They should be required, under a penalty, to limit the amount of their debts, whether to note-holders oı depositors, in proportion to their specie.

But, of all regulations, no one has been found more beneficial than frequent published statements of their condition; in which the amount of their loans, circulation, deposits, and specie should be officially stated. At fixed times, also, commissioners should be appointed by the Government, to make a strict examination and full report of their liabilities and resources.

With these and other similar restrictions, as experience should develope their necessity, the public would be more effectually guarded against the imprudence of these institutions than they can be by the plan which has lately obtained public favor under the name of "free banks," by which those institutions are deprived of the power of creating a paper currency, but may obtain notes for circulation from the Government on depositing with the proper public authorities approved stock of the States to an equal amount, as eventual security for the redemption of the notes. It has been found by experience that the plan does not prevent the banks from suspending specie payments like the rest; and so far, they have failed in one of their most important objects. It is also well known that if, in consequence of the embarrassment of the banks, the stock pledged by them should be thrown into the market, it would sell greatly under par, and thus fail to redeem the notes for which it had been pledged. It must, however, be admitted that, in the reckless way in which bank charters have often been granted, and in which both the stockholders and directors have commonly performed their respective duties, this plan of banking affords some security against those very heavy losses which the public has sometimes sustained from those institutions.

That portion of the capital of a community which consists of money, though it is often denominated its *circulation*, more properly falls under the head of *fixed* than of *circulating* capital. It is not, like the former, consumed by a single use, but may exercise its useful functions again and again until it is worn out. It may, in its faculty of facilitating exchanges, be assimilated to wagons or other carriages used for transportation, and, like them, its wear and tear is the amount of its annual cost to the nation.

Some persons, in consideration of the frequent failure of banks to redeem their notes, and of the serious mischiefs to the community which thence ensue, would substitute banks of deposit for banks of circulation, to furnish a safe paper currency, since they have specie in their vaults for every note they have issued, and consequently their notes, thus certain to be redeemed, furnish the public with a paper circulation of equal value with gold and silver, and which can never depreciate.

To this proposition there is more than one objection. The first is that it would deprive the community of the advantage now enjoyed of the gain derived from the substitution of so cheap an article as paper for the precious metals, and which constitutes an important item of national economy. It is fair to assume that, if there were no bank paper in circulation, there would be a specie currency to nearly the same amount. Let us suppose the excess of paper to be 10 per cent. The amount of bank paper, thus reduced, would not be less than two hundred millions. To save this amount of capital, however expended, whether in productive or unproductive consumption, has always been considered a great national benefit; consequently, to surrender it, and retracing our steps by buying from other countries as much gold and silver as would supply the place of our present paper circulation, would be a far more serious injury. Even if executed very slowly and gradually, so large a demand for new capital would cause a pressure beyond endurance. It would have the same effect, for the time, as the annihilation of capital to the same amount as the substitution, and it would equally arrest useful enterprise, and paralyze every species of profitable industry.

But, in the next place, if the plan could be carried into execution, its promised benefits would not probably be of long continuance. In a bank of deposit, like that of Amsterdam, the specie would be steadily accumulating until, if not interfered with, it would amount to nearly the whole circulating currency of the country. But in this process it would always be exposed to more than one danger. When those who had the charge of this treasure (supposing them incapable of abstracting any of it for their own purposes), found that it had long lain idle and untouched, would be tempted to afford pecuniary relief to others, especially public bodies and corporations, as was done by the Bank of Amsterdam, under the delusive expectation that the money could be returned whenever it should be actually wanted. And though the managers of the bank should be proof against all such temptations, yet public sentiment itself might produce the same result; and, in any season of public difficulty or emergency, such as invasion, insurrection, or war, they might insist on making a part of the idle hoards of the bank active and useful in aiding the public treasury—in which case, the specie retained in the bank being still sufficient to redeem the notes returned to it, the bank of deposit would be converted into a bank of circulation, if it continued to exist, or its business was not altogether closed.

We have seen that the production of any commodity may be excessive, or, in other words, that its supply may exceed its demand. But while this is very practicable for one or several commodities, it can never be the case with all. Since commodities are purchased by commodities, the glut of some always supposes a deficiency of others. A general excess is, therefore, a contradiction, as has been well shown by Mr. Say in his theory of gluts.

Having now gone through the subject of production of what is necessary or useful to man, whether by agriculture, mining, fisheries, manufactures, or com merce, we will proceed to consider the destination of what has been thus produced.

CHAPTER XIV.

CONSUMPTION.

THE end and object of all production is consumption; for why should men exert bodily toil or mental care in producing, except for the gratification afforded by consuming, or using what had been produced. His productive industry has, therefore, always been conducted with a view to this result. Thus, let us look to the production of a loaf of bread. After the land has been cleared of its timber, or other spontaneous growth, it must be broken up by the plough or the spade. It must then be sowed with the seed sought to be multiplied — say wheat, and harrowed. It germinates, grows, and finally ripens, when it is reaped by one instrument or machine; threshed out by another, and winnowed by a third. It is then carried to the mill, where it is first ground into flour, which is separated into two or three kinds, and all of them from the bran. The flour is carried to the baker, who, by a process, partly mechanical and partly chemical, makes it into dough, kneads and bakes it, when it becomes one of the most common articles of human subsistence.

In like manner of a beef-steak. The ox from

which it was taken was probably reared in a region where the natural herbage was abundant. He was thence transported to a distance, where he was purchased and fattened for the shambles. He was then killed by the butcher, who distributed his flesh, hide, hair, tallow, feet, bones, and horns to different sets of customers, for their several purposes, and one of the most savory portions of his meat was conveyed to the cook, who converted it into a steak. And so with every object of apparel, from a hat to a shoe, or of household furniture, from a grand piano to a kitchen-fork.

Of the immense multitude of articles thus annually produced for man's necessities or gratification, the whole is consumed in about the same time that it has been produced, with the exception of a small portion,—about five or six per cent.,—which gradually adds to the wealth of the community.

This consumption, however, is not made altogether by the individuals who were the producers; but a considerable portion is made by the community, in its aggregate character—that is, by the Government. This distribution is very different in different countries; and as a general rule, the larger the share which is received by individuals, and the smaller that received by the Government, the happier and freer are the people.

The better to understand how the portion consumed by the Government is separated from the whole amount annually produced and disbursed, let us advert to the distribution of political power.

In all well-organized governments, the power of the state is, by its fundamental principles, or constitution, divided between the legislature, the executive, and the judiciary. The legislature determines its own ordinary functions, as well as those of the executive and judiciary. It controls the conduct of individuals when the public good requires it, enjoining some acts, and prohibiting others. It provides for the national defence, by sea and land. It maintains a friendly diplomatic intercourse with foreign nations. It establishes courts to administer justice and to punish crimes, prescribes the rules of property and of civil rights, and lastly, it provides an adequate revenue, which is disbursed in the modes and according to the rules it has prescribed.

The executive has the power of appointing all officers, civil, military, or naval. By these it defends the country against foreign enemies or domestic insurrection, collects and disburses the public revenue, and executes the judgments of the courts, both civil and criminal.

The judiciary, however, tries all public offenders, and sentences them to punishment. It settles all disputes between individuals about property, enforces contracts, maintains rights, whether derived from law or custom, and decides all questions by settled rules of evidence, and in accordance with the behests of law and the principles of justice.

To enable the Government to perform these high and important duties, the legislature must provide an adequate revenue, which is sometimes derived in part from the profits or sales of public property, but mainly from taxes, the principles of which we will now consider; premising that, inasmuch as by far the larger part of every community spend on themselves and their families all their earnings, this subject of taxation is a very important one, as respects both the productiveness of the tax and the interest of the people.

According to Adam Smith, whose views on this subject have been generally approved, taxes ought to conform to the four following maxims:

1. Every citizen ought to contribute to the public revenue in proportion to his ability. It is sheer justice that he who has the largest amount of property protected should pay the most for that protection.

2. The tax which each person is required to pay should be certain, both as to the amount, the time, and the mode of payment; so as to leave as little discretion as possible to the tax-gatherer. The uncertainty of a tax is severely felt by the payer, as it prevents preparation, or makes it unavailing, though it may add nothing to the revenue.

3. Every tax ought to be levied at the time and in the mode which is most convenient to the payer.

A tax, for example, on articles as consumpted, may be very little felt, while the same tax, collected at once, might be oppressive, and perhaps impracticable.

4. A tax should take out, and keep out, of the pocket of the payer, as little as possible beyond what it brings into the public treasury. Thus, a tax may pass through several successive hands, each of whom, receiving his compensation proportionally, deducts from the proceeds of the tax. It may, by prohibiting or discouraging particular branches of industry, render many persons less able to pay the tax. It may, by encouraging smuggling, and evasions of the tax, render it less productive. It may tax the time as well as the purses of the citizens. And lastly, it may subject the citizen to the interruption and vexation of domiciliary visits and inquisition.

Taxes are sometimes used for other purposes than revenue. When laid on what are regarded as nuisances, they are meant to be prohibitions, and, when they fail in this object, to make to the public some compensation for the failure. Of this character are taxes on gaming and drinking-houses, or lotteries.

They are also meant, by discouraging one branch of industry, to encourage another: as where a tax is laid on certain fabrics received from abroad by the exchanges of commerce, for the sake of encouraging the domestic producer of similar articles, on whose industry the tax operates as a bounty.

The preceding views will be illustrated by a separate notice of the taxes which are principally resorted to for revenue.

The Land Tax.—As the land of every civilized and populous community constitutes the largest item of its property—is the main source of its annual income, and cannot be withdrawn from the reach of the tax-gatherers—it is a general object of taxation, and source of public revenue.

This tax should vary in its rate, according to the value of the land. This rule is, in some measure, necessary as well as just. An uniform tax, if not very low, would be more than poor lands could pay; and, if it were low, it could not yield much.

Nor would it be right to apportion this tax according to the income yielded by the land; since city lots and unimproved lands, though they might yield no direct income, might compensate their proprietors by the steady increase of their value, and property, although thus productive, would escape taxation. The fairest rule, then, would be to tax land according to its market value, which would comprehend its obvious future as well as its present capabilities. But here again injustice may be done. It is not unusual for one person to have a life estate in landed property, and another the reversion; and although the former, who receives the present profit, ought to pay the largest share, the other ought not to be wholly exempt. To adjust the tax equitably between them would be a matter of some difficulty, and would probably admit of no rule that would not be sometimes unjust to one of the parties. The foregoing considerations seem to make a land tax ineligible, unless it is a very light one.

But another objection to this tax in the United States is that, as the value of land is greatly increased by the increased density of population, it is liable to very great and rapid changes here; so as for it to have any foundation in justice, there must be frequent valuations, which occasion a heavy expense, and one of frequent occurrence. The land tax, however the landed proprietor may appear to succeed in throwing it on his tenant, must always fall upon himself, and must be deducted from the annual profits of the land.

Tax on houses.—This tax falls wholly or principally on their tenants. Houses must yield the ordinary profits of capital, or they will not be supplied — and if their annual charge is raised, whether by a tax or in any other way, the rent must rise in proportion, except in those cities and towns that are going to decay, when the supply of houses may exceed the demand — in which case the tax must fall upon the proprietor, and be taken from the rent.

Tax on imports.—This tax is recommended by so many considerations, that by far the greater part of the revenue of the General Government is raised in this way. As it is laid on articles of general consumption, such as sugar, coffee, tea, wine, and every species of woven goods, it is in general paid by the citizens according to their ability, because according to their ordinary expenses. It is more productive than any other tax could be, since by reason of the large amount of our imports, a moderate impost will yield a large revenue. It being collected by the respective custom-houses at the places of import, and paid in large sums by the importing merchant, it costs less to collect it than any other tax; and lastly, it encourages the domestic production of many commodities, by subjecting the fabrics of their foreign rivals to an additional cost. Without this tax, many branches of domestic manufacture, and some few of raw produce, which are now thriving and profitable, would be greatly diminished, and some would be abandoned altogether. Whether this is a national advantage or not, is another question, which has been discussed in another place.*

Its disadvantages, though small, compared with its benefits, must also be noticed. First, the tax invites to smuggling, which, as it can be carried on in retired creeks and inlets, can be prevented, or rather checked, only by revenue cutters, maintained at a great expense — or by officers placed along the line which separates the United States from the British colonies on this continent. Secondly, by unduly encouraging particular branches of industry, it causes capital and labor to be diverted from a more profitable employment, and thus causes a loss of the national capital;

---

* See page 116.

and lastly, because all those who abstain from the use of imported merchandise may exempt themselves from the payment of any portion of the tax.

Excise.—This term is commonly applied to a tax or duty on home-made articles; and, like the impost, is paid by the consumer of the articles, who, in purchasing them, pays the tax. It is occasionally extended to a great variety of articles, but in this country has commonly been confined to the distiller of spirits, which are taxed partly because their consumption is regarded as unfavorable both to the health and the morals of the people, and partly because, on account of the prevalent popular taste for them, the tax is very productive.

The objection to this class of taxes is, that to insure its faithful collection, many officers are necessary, with a course of inquisition which is vexatious and repugnant to the feelings of a free people. The first excise laid in the United States caused an insurrection in the western part of Pennsylvania—the people there regarding it as peculiarly oppressive and unjust, since whiskey was the only product of their industry which would then bear the expense of transportation to market, by reason of which the tax fell more heavily on their industry than on any other in the Union. The objection would have been well founded, but for the fact that the tax on spirits, though advanced by the manufacturer, would eventually fall on the consumer. The same tax has been subsequently laid, and has not been unacceptable to the distillers of spirits.

Stamp Taxes.—This is a tax which is levied on such papers and documents as are of frequent use in the business transactions of men, as deeds, bonds, agreements, receipts, etc.; and to enforce the payment of the tax, all such papers are not permitted to be used as evidence in a court of justice, and are thus deprived of the principal benefit for which they had been created. One objection to this class of taxes is that they operate very unequally—it not being always practicable to graduate the tax according to the value or importance of the subject matter of the stamped paper, so that a paper concerning a value of $100 may pay as much as $10,000. But a more serious objection to such taxes in this country is that they are often not merely a tax on the purse, but a much heavier one on the time of the citizen. In retired country places, a man, instead of writing a bond or receipt on the first piece of paper that is at hand, may be compelled to go or send ten or twelve miles for a stamp.

Taxes on Banks.—As these corporations are invested with the valuable privilege of substituting their paper for specie, from which the citizens are generally interdicted, and as, moreover, there is always danger that they may bring on the community the evil of a depreciated currency, it is just and right that they should contribute toward defraying the expenses of the Government. They may do this by paying a bonus for their charter, or by an annual tax on their dividends; and sometimes a tax has been laid on their loans, which, however, always falls on their borrowers.

Taxes on Auctions. — This tax seems to be recommended partly because it is not easily evaded, since the auctioneers are commonly responsible for the tax, and partly by way of discouragement, as many are induced to purchase at auction what they do not need, and what they would not otherwise have bought.

Capitation, or Poll Taxes. — These, from their simplicity, were formerly much resorted to; but since, when they are uniform, they cannot yield much, and when they vary with the fortunes of individuals they are unequal, and leave much to the discretion of the collectors, they are now but little used in this country.

Taxes are sometimes levied by means of licenses, to consume wine, coffee, and tea, or to follow a particular occupation — as to keep a tavern, to be a merchant, a pedler, an auctioneer, to keep a billiard saloon, etc.

The objection to these taxes is that they are often very unequal. There was formerly, in Virginia, a tax on merchants' licences, which was the same on each individual, whether his capital or business was large or small. They are commonly recommended by the consideration that a tax is in this way collected from persons who would otherwise escape taxation.

Taxes on necessaries fall at first on labor, but eventually on all classes. Taxes on luxuries fall exclusively on the rich or the ostentatious.

Taxes have been divided into direct and indirect —that is, those in which the tax is directly collected from the citizen, and those in which the tax laid on an article in the hands of the producer or importer enters into its price, and is thus paid by the consumer when he purchases the article.

It has often been maintained by politicians that direct taxes were preferable to indirect, on two grounds: 1. That they are more economical; and 2. That, being more felt, they are a check on the extravagance and ambition of governments. The preference claimed for direct taxes may, however, well be impugned. The argument that they are more economical rests mainly on this—that indirect taxes, being advanced by the importer or home producer, he must be paid for such advance, and the taxed commodity is thereby the dearer to the consumer. The guards, too, to prevent evasions of the indirect tax, are a heavy expense, from which direct taxes are exempt.

There may be countries in which direct taxes can be levied at less expense than the indirect; but it is not the case in the United States. Here, whenever a direct tax is laid, it must be apportioned among the States according to their representation in Congress, and the property taxed must be valued. Now, the cost of such valuation renders this mode of taxation about eight times as costly as the impost; and from the rapid changes in the value of the lands here, their valuation would have to be repeated as often as the tax was laid.

But if indirect taxes were less economical, they would be far more eligible. They are paid at the time and in the mode that is most easy to every one, who pays the tax in purchasing those things that he finds most to his taste and gratification. It is one of the first duties of a government to draw its necessary revenue from the people in that way which is the least onerous; and that is, by indirect taxes. To regard the greater pressure and disagreeableness of a tax as a recommendation, seems to be as wise as it would be to make our food distasteful in order to save us from the danger of gluttony or excess. Every prudent and considerate government, therefore, prefers indirect taxes as long as they are adequate to the public wants.

Another objection to direct taxes is, that it is not only more inconvenient for the citizen to pay the whole amount of his taxes at once rather than by little at a time, as he purchases the taxed articles, but it also requires a much larger addition to the circulating medium of the country; and in preparing to pay it, a portion of his funds must be long unemployed.

Taxes are sometimes laid on the property of the deceased, especially when it is bequeathed to collateral relations. This, in general, is a tax that is little felt by the payer; but it would often fall on property scarce able to pay the tax in addition to the other charges with which it was previously burthened; in which case, it might be a tax on productive capital.

We will now advert to the principal modes in which the public revenue is expended—and first, for the national defence.

By the art of war, and the aid of arms, especially the invention of gunpowder, the destructive powers of man have been so increased, that one thousand well-equipped soldiers may vanquish and destroy an hundred times their number, provided with only the natural means of defence. Experience teaches us that those who possess this superiority are not slow to use and abuse it. Nations, therefore, to preserve their independence, have found it necessary to cultivate the same means of destruction; hence have arisen, sometimes for defence and sometimes for offence, armed associations of men, at first for short terms, then for longer ones, and finally permanent or standing armies. But inasmuch as these have sometimes been used by their ambitious leaders to destroy the liberties they were created to preserve, they have naturally become objects of jealousy with free nations. They are fortunately, however, not necessary to the defence of such nations. Familiarized as their people commonly are to the use of firearms, and though but slightly instructed by the militia laws to act in masses, they are a surer and stronger means of national defense than any standing army can be. In a season of danger or emergency, their volunteers will soon form an army more numerous and more brave, because more patriotic, than mere mercenaries are ever likely to be — as was experienced by the United States in the late Mexican War.

It was formerly supposed that no nation could support a permanent military force exceeding one hundredth part of its population; and though, with the aid derived from modern improvements in the means of feeding, clothing, and arming its military force, some nations have exceeded this limit, the excess has not been great, and has proved very oppressive to their people.

The naval power of maritime nations is a still more efficient means of defence than the army. This species of armament is likely to be materially affected by the application of steam-power, but the precise character of this change has not yet been determined by experience.

The other disbursements of the government are mainly in the pay of its civil officers of all descriptions.

CHAPTER XV.

PUBLIC DEBTS.

But it sometimes happens that a nation is urged to incur expenses to which its ordinary revenue is inadequate. It is called upon to resist an invasion by foreign enemies, or to suppress a serious domestic insurrection. These occurrences at once lessen the resources of the State at the very time that the demands upon them are increased. On such occasions they, like individuals, have recourse to borrowing, to obtain the means of meeting the emergencies of the time. Even the increased expenses attending a war may recommend to the government recourse to a loan for its extraordinary expenses, in preference to new taxes.

There are other modes in which a public debt may originate. In the ordinary transactions of most governments it is often found convenient to give, instead of money to the officers and agents of the government, written evidences of their claims for public services; and where these claims have been suffered to accumulate, in consequence of pressing demands on the public treasury, they have at length become a recognised public debt. and the government has contented itself with the payment of an annual interest, for which it makes a permanent provision. This is what is called *funding* the debt. In this way the exchequer and navy bills in England have been often funded. A debt may also be contracted by the purchase of territory of a foreign government. In this way the United States contracted a debt for the purchase of Louisiana. So of the money which they contracted to pay to Mexico for the cession of territory by the treaty of 1848.

This expedient enables a modern State, in the stability and good faith of whose government the world has confidence, greatly to extend its power, whether for protection or offence, and the money thus procured may be not only much more than could be obtained by taxes, but it is obtained much more speedily, and is commonly that part of the national capital which yields the least profit. Thus, the British Government, where the ordinary interest is 5 per cent., can commonly borrow millions at an interest of 3½ per cent., or even less; and the United States, where the market rate of interest is from 7 to 10 per cent. in the different States, would find no difficulty in borrowing at 5 per cent.

The way in which the money thus borrowed is expended, may most essentially contribute to the defence of the nation, and even to its interests, but the national capital is not on that account the less impaired. Every public loan must, in lightening the present burdens of the government, add to those of posterity; and when the debt goes on steadily increasing, as it often does, the annual taxes required to pay the interest of the debt, may be sufficient in amount to defray the whole of the other expenses of the government. Every public loan is thus apt to be the parent of new debt, as it adds to the annual public expenditure. Hence there is a strong tendency for public debts, after once begun, to go on increasing; and the United States furnish the only example of a large public debt being fully and honestly discharged.

The public debt of a country is an exponent of what, on considerations of high public policy, may have been wisely and beneficially expended; yet, in an economical view, it must always represent a diminution of the active productive capital of the country.

Let us not, however, overrate the national loss, even when viewed under this aspect. Much which has been spent by armies and navies, would have been as unproductively spent if the same capital had remained in the hands of individuals; and it is the same thing to the wealth of the nation, whether the money has been expended in paying soldiers and sailors, or in feeding a pack of hounds, or maintaining a costly equipage and long retinue of servants. Besides, a portion of the money expended on the naval and military service employs and rewards productive industry in providing food, clothing, arms, and ammunition—all of which make not an insignificant deduction from the amount of the national revenue spent by the government.

But while, after every deduction is made, the destruction of the national capital, indicated by the public debt, is very great, it does not so seriously threaten the safety, or even the resources of the States, as has been often supposed.

Whenever the loan is made by the citizens of the country making it, as is often done, then it being made from the savings of the excess of production over consumption, the money was earned before it was spent, and it is thus drawn from the profits of previous industry. So long as loans are made in this way, from the capitals already accumulated, it is not easy to set limits to their amount—since taxes, both direct and indirect, to pay the increasing interest, may be made to reach the public creditor as well as others. Thus the ruinous consequences which have been often predicted of public debts seem to be altogether fallacious, though their injurious effects are undeniable; and since, in return for the present benefit they may afford, they must always lessen the means of individual comfort or gratification, and impair the sources of public revenue, they ought never to be resorted to except on occasions of great national urgency; and should be paid off as soon as the revenue of the State is sufficiently productive.

Governments have resorted to different expedients to relieve themselves from the burden of debt. Sometimes they have depreciated the coin, sometimes they have, by paying neither principal nor interest, occasioned the evidences of the debt to depreciate, and have then profited by that depreciation, and redeemed the public debt, by paying a small part of its original amount. Sometimes, again, they have committed an open act of bankruptcy or repudiation, and have either disavowed the whole debt, or paid a small portion of it. The United States present the only example of the payment of their entire debt without any deduction.

Besides the debts formally contracted by the Government, it may happen that one country may owe a large debt to another, in the course of their commercial and other dealings. The country which has the least capital is always likely to be in debt to the country which has the most. The money which is then paid for interest is often regarded as an ignominious tribute, and as a serious national loss. Yet it may easily happen that the indebted nation gains more than it loses by the use of the capital it has borrowed. Thus, suppose that it borrows at an interest of five per cent., and that the market rate is eight per cent. This indicates a probable gain of three per cent.

When a merchant or manufacturer has a reasonable expectation of making a profit from the use of borrowed capital, it is of no importance in a national point of view whether he borrow the money at home or abroad. It is better, both for him and the community, that he obtain it where it can be got on the best terms.

If the borrowed money was invested in an unprofitable undertaking, as in an ill-advised and unproductive railroad, then, indeed, it would be a national loss, though not greater than if it had been borrowed at home.

CHAPTER XVI.

THE PUBLIC EXPENDITURE.

Of those establishments required by the public welfare which the Government alone is competent to provide, the following are the principal:

An army to repel foreign invasions, or to suppress domestic insurrection.

Fortifications are also required in places accessible to ships in particular situations in the interior. Repositories of arms and ammunition, and manufactories of cannon and other implements of war, are also important, as well as schools of instruction for engineers and other officers. A navy, too, consisting of ships, steamers, gun-boats, etc., should be provided, as a most efficient means of national defence, together with a large supply of seasoned timber, and of manufactured iron, adapted to naval structures; provision for diplomatic intercourse with foreign nations, by means of ambassadors, ministers, and consuls; also officers and offices for the collection and safe keeping of the revenue, whether by impost, excise, or the survey and sales of public lands; for coining money at the mint, for the payment of pensions to those who have been disabled or superannuated in the public service, and for the management of the post-office.

Of this description are jails and penitentiaries for the safe-keeping and punishment of criminals. The latter are thought greatly to tend to prevent crimes, by affording ready means of graduating punishments to offences, and by making them more certain — it being found that when the smaller offences, as well as the great, were made capital, both courts and juries were often astute in acquitting those who had been guilty of the less heinous felonies.

There are other important establishments, which are furnished wholly by the State governments, or in some cases partly by them, with the co-operation of individuals; among the most important are those of religion.

In most countries, religion is established by the authority of the state. Its creed and mode of worship are prescribed, and the support of its ministers is provided for by law. But in the United States, every one's religious faith and worship are left to his own conscience. He may make contribution to any sect, little or much, or he may refuse it altogether.

This liberality seems to be clearly sanctioned by the principles of justice. Of the various kinds of religious faith which prevail in the world, it seems clear that at least ninety-nine in a hundred belong to the one in which they have been educated; and we may confidently pronounce a man or woman to be a Catholic or Protestant, an Episcopalian, Presbyterian, Methodist, or Baptist, according to the persuasion of their parents, or those by whom they were brought up; and in the hundredth case (of exception to the rule), the deviation may be traced to the influence of some ascendant mind, or that of some eloquent tract; so that the new tenets thus acquired have been the result of accident or chance, for which the holder seems to be as little responsible as for a disease caused by the changes of the atmosphere.

The same liberal course is recommended by policy. It has been found that wherever there has been a rule of faith prescribed by law, there will be many dissentients, whom the supporters of the national creed will be disposed to proscribe and perhaps persecute; and, though the power of the law may not be pushed to that extreme, there will be between the favored sect and the rest perpetual jealousy and discord, very hostile to that charity which all good religions inculcate. No wars have been so bitter and implacable as those which have grown out of religious controversy; and this abuse of power is so natural, that those who have at one time been the victims of persecution, have, on the attainment of power, become persecutors themselves.

Several theoretical objections have been made to the footing on which religion is placed in the United States. It was first supposed that where there was no legal restraint on religious controversy, it would be more frequent and violent. But experience has shown that, where all sects enjoy equal freedom and privileges, there will be harmony, or at least no disturbance of the public peace.

It being found that the first objection had been completely falsified, it was then urged that religious zeal, not having here the stimulants and support which prevail in other countries, would gradually languish and die. But this prediction has been equally contradicted by experience. The emulation among the different sects for popular favor and success, has been found sufficient to produce as much fervor in this country as in any other. The entire dependence of every minister on his congregation for his worldly support, as well as for his efficiency, has an obvious influence on his zeal, his diligence, and outward deportment; and the people exercise their acknowledged power of censorship earnestly and unremittingly. There is no country where the ministers of religion are more moral, more attentive to the decorums of life, or exercise more practical charity—none in which they allow themselves less latitude of personal indulgence.

In the third place, it was presumed that the clergy would not be sufficiently provided for when they were wholly dependent on voluntary contribution. But it is found that the number of churches and of persons composing their congregations is as great here as it is in most countries of Europe; and, although no ministers here receive as large salaries as are received there by the higher dignitaries of the church, most of them obtain more liberal remuneration than the great body of the European clergy. A moderate but competent salary is more favorable to true and heartfelt piety than either an overgrown income, so likely to nourish ambition, vanity, and self-indulgence, or a very small one, in which the pressure of want may engross the thoughts and cares of the minister.

Lastly, it has been supposed that the entire dependence of every religious minister on the contributions of his congregation would beget in him a time-serving spirit, and check that free animadversion on immorality and vice which is one of his highest duties as well as most important services. But here, again, experience lends its refutation. It is found that there is no way in which a preacher can so well recommend himself to his flock as by an earnest and uncompromising denunciation of moral delinquency and vice, provided it be not personal; and no one could take umbrage at censures of this general character without bringing himself into discredit.

It seems not improbable that the entire freedom of religion is favorable to the multiplication of sects. Whenever the ambition of being the founder of a sect, the desire of celebrity, or the mere love of novelty prompts a minister to promulgate new doctrines, or to recommend new forms of worship, he has much to encourage him in his purpose in the unrestrained freedom which prevails here in all matters of conscience; and if he has eloquence as well as zeal, he sometimes becomes the founder of a sect which bears his name.

A question has sometimes arisen whether, when the doctrines or practice of a religious sect are directly opposed to the admitted policy of the country, or to the national habits and manners, these irregularities were not amenable to the laws. This is a question of great delicacy, and is always likely to offend that sense of religious freedom which the fundamental laws of the State secure to every man. The case of the Mormons, in the territory of Utah, whose religion permits, and even enjoins, polygamy, has especially suggested this question to the American people; and the general Government may be soon called upon to act on it.

The polygamy thus sanctioned and practised by them is not only abhorrent to the manners of the people in all the States, but it is punished by them as a high crime. Although it may be deemed incompatible with the rights of popular sovereignty, as well as of religious freedom, to attempt to put down this practice by force, or by penalties, yet the other States may be well justified in refusing to admit into their confederacy a community which openly justifies, under the authority of religion, a practice which they consider so repugnant to morality, purity of manners, and social happiness. Not to concede this, would be to make the Mormons not merely the equals, but the superiors of other States, in extending to them the same toleration for their crimes as their rights. The power of granting to a community admission into the Union implies the right of rejection whenever such considerations as the national liberty, the national morality, or happiness require it.

CHAPTER XVII.

EDUCATION.

Of all the political institutions which the wit of man has devised, none seems to be of so much importance as those which provide for juvenile instruction. The duties of a citizen in a civilized community are so multifarious, and many of them require so much previous training, that, unless a considerable portion of his early life is given to the preparation, he is incapable of performing many of the most important duties and offices of a citizen. We may form some idea of the value of this instruction by comparing a well-educated man with one who can neither write nor read.

But education not only adds to a man's stock of knowledge, both of matter and mind, but is also favorable to his morals. Experience teaches us that, in all communities where the people are generally instructed, they are remarkably exempt from crime; and, though it may often happen that those persons whose minds have been much cultivated are depraved and unprincipled, and have yielded to the fascinations of some seductive vice; yet these must be regarded as exceptions to the general rule. A taste for literature and science affords one of the best securities against the temptations to vicious indulgence, and cherishes the generous ambition to acquire the approbation and esteem of other men.

Mental acquirements also afford profitable employment to numbers who possess no other capital than their intellects. How many thousands of our clergymen, physicians, lawyers, and others, earn liberal incomes, and obtain a high station in society, who started in life without a penny, and, in some cases, without a friend! It is not only from the educated class that our statesmen, legislators, and chief public functionaries are furnished, but likewise all those who fill the learned professions, or who conduct the press, and even our military and naval affairs. When education is so indispensable to the community, and can effectuate so much for individuals, it is no wonder that it is one of the first concerns of an intelligent people, and that millions are set apart to defray its expense. It is thus regarded as the highest eulogy which can be bestowed on any government, whether it be a republic or monarchy, that it has an efficient system of juvenile instruction.

The various and diverse duties of an individual in a community seem to divide it into three classes: one for the great mass of the people, whose chief occupation is that of physical labor, or of household service; the second for those who require a higher degree of knowledge of men and things in discharging the duties of agriculturists, merchants, and artificers; and lastly, colleges and universities, in which a yet higher degree of science is taught, to fit men for the more difficult duties of the higher offices of government, and of the learned professions.

In the first class, the elementary schools, the child should be taught to read and write, the rudiments of arithmetic, geography, and practical geometry, and, if possible, of physical science. It is of especial importance in a republic that this class, comprehending the great body of voters, should be instructed, that they may not only learn, through the press, the opinions of the men for whom they are called upon to vote, but be better able to judge of the soundness of those opinions, as well as of the other qualifications of the candidates. These schools should be supported at the people's expense, with the aid of those who could afford contributions.

The second class, that of academies, should also receive some support from the public treasury, but be dependent principally on the contributions of those who profit by them. The subjects taught here should be chiefly classical learning and mathematics, and, in part for those who would there finish their education, the most useful branches of physical science.

The third class, that of colleges and universities, should afford opportunity to acquire every branch of learning and science. These higher schools should be provided at the public expense, be furnished with a complete apparatus, and the requisite materials for experiments, with ample libraries, with museums of the diversified products of nature, mineral, animal, and vegetable, and lastly, with a fund for the compensation of professors, sufficient to secure the services of the ablest men; and, to stimulate their unremitting industry, their emolument should be derived partly from a fixed salary, and partly from the fees paid by their respective students.

It is found in the United States that the number of those now taught in the primary or elementary schools is about ten or twelve times as many as those taught in the academies; and that the latter are nearly ten times the number of college students.

In 1850, according to the census, there were 234 colleges and universities in the United States. The number of students attending them was 27,159. When it is recollected that the greater part of those students continue two or three years at college, so as to make the whole number annually educated not more than ten or twelve thousand—that if we farther deduct from this number those who are neither office-holders nor professional men, and those who prematurely die, the residue bears so small a proportion to the whole class of those who were supported by mental industry, including the higher public officers, which was 179,000—it may be fairly inferred that a large majority of the public officers and professional men have not received a college education.

In our notice of this subject, we must not overlook the education of females. When we consider how large a share mothers have in forming the minds and morals of their children, and how many great men have owed their eminence to maternal teaching and influence, we must be satisfied that female instruction must have a most important bearing on the improvement and prosperity of a State. The seminaries and boarding-schools for the education of females have greatly multiplied of late years, and are steadily increasing. But the prevalent systems of female education seem to be defective in this, that they set a higher value on mere accomplishments that may give a transient distinction, than on those solid qualifications which best fit females for the performance of the high duties assigned to them.

These duties are to manage a household prudently and efficiently; to be the intelligent counsellor, as well as agreeable companion of the partner of their fortunes; to develop and improve the mental faculties and moral propensities of their offspring. To such elevated attributes, skill in music, drawing, or dancing, though they too are not without their use, are of subordinate importance. Nor should the education of a female be considered complete without some knowledge of chemistry, so far as it is applicable to the ordinary concerns of life, and to the details of practical cookery, which is of so much value to our health, to our comfort, and to a proper economy. The use of the needle seems to be so indispensable that it is rarely ever neglected, though much of the heaviest part of this labor is now fortunately consigned to machinery.

There are some professions and trades from which women have been hitherto excluded, but for which they seem to be entirely competent. They are well qualified for some branches of the medical art, especially for the diseases of their own sex; and they are peculiarly adapted to the office of nursing, which, in many diseases, when associated with intelligence, affords the most efficient aid that can be given. They are also excellent shop-keepers; are as efficient as men in the business of printing, book-binding, in some branches of jewelry, and in every branch of making clothes. They seem perfectly competent to exercise the profession of painting, engraving, and other branches of the imitative arts; and, for the business of juvenile instruction, their gentleness, patience, and delicate sympathy, peculiarly fit them, since the stimulus of the desire to learn, which they are so skilled in calling forth, is much more efficacious than that of fear, to which male teachers so frequently appeal.

A system of general juvenile instruction, comprehending the youth of both sexes, cannot be too much cherished by a wise community. Under its expansive and growing influence a nation would be continually advancing in knowledge, in power over brute matter, in the means of happiness, and in moral dignity.

On the subject of improving the intelligence of a people, we cannot overlook the agency of the periodical press. By its communicating to all who can read, on terms that are within the reach of the poorest classes of the community, every man can obtain a knowledge of all important events and facts, not only in his own country, but almost of every other, immediately after they have occurred; and, although the newspapers sometimes give currency to what is false, yet they probably circulate an hundred times as much truth as falsehood. They are thus adding to that knowledge of men and things which is generally acquired only by observation and experience. They afford daily gratification to man's love of novelty; save many not only from *ennui*, but from vicious indulgences; and do much to superinduce a taste for reading and intellectual improvement.

CHAPTER XVIII.

PUBLIC CHARITIES.

In every country, however rich or prosperous, the great mass of the people have an expenditure which is equal to their income, and is not easily capable of reduction. They are, of course, unprepared for those diseases or sinister casualties that put an end to their daily earnings, either permanently or for the time. Humanity then requires that provision should be made for the relief of those who are thus afflicted, out of the revenues of the more fortunate classes. Hospitals are therefore provided with adequate funds, and are placed under the management of a competent and permanent board of directors.

The class of persons whose misfortunes thus address themselves to the sympathies of the community are the blind, the deaf and dumb, the insane, those who have been maimed, or afflicted with diseases that unfit them for labor, and lastly, those who are too poor for the maintenance of themselves and their families; which last class will require a separate consideration.

Of the claims of the four first classes to relief,

there can be no doubt; and the only question is as to the extent and mode of assistance.

Though there is not entire uniformity in the proportion of persons thus afflicted, yet the diversity appears to be not very great; and it would seem, from the decennial census of the population of the United States and of other countries, that about one in 2000 persons is probably blind, that the proportion of the deaf and dumb is the same, and that one in 1000 is insane; making, in the three classes, three in 5000—equivalent to six-tenths of one per cent. of the whole population. The number of those who are incapable of supporting themselves either by their labor or capital, in consequence of being maimed or diseased, is not ascertained; but it is probably much larger than that of either of the other classes. If we suppose it to be as much as two in the 1000, it would make the whole number who have undeniable claims to the public charity reach five in the 5000, or one per cent of the whole population; which imposes not a burthensome charge on the community.

The claim, however, of those who are merely poor, but who have experienced neither disease nor infirmity to disqualify them for bodily labor, is another question.

It has been contended by many, ever since Mr. Malthus's work on the tendency of mankind, by their increase, to press on the means of subsistence, that a general system of providing relief for those who are merely poor, tends to increase the very evil it aimed to remedy; and that if individuals, regardless of those considerations of prudence which should prevent them from encumbering themselves with families without possessing the means of their support, and the public should be ready to supply the relief needed by such imprudence, then one of the most efficient checks to redundancy of numbers would be taken away; that cases of such improvident marriages would probably be multiplied, and the evils of poverty and want be thereby augmented; that, consequently, the only system which will keep down population to the level of comfortable subsistence, is to let the imprudent take the consequences of their own error, rather than to cast its results on the rest of the community.

The principle that population will always be in proportion to the means of subsistence had been propounded by Sir James Steuart, Adam Smith, Dr. Franklin, and probably others, long before Mr. Malthus; but he was the first who traced its influence on human welfare. While I readily admit the ability and value of Mr. Malthus's work, it has long appeared to me that he has somewhat overrated the multiplying propensity of mankind, which I do not think too strong, and has undervalued the checks to redundancy.*

* These propositions are made by the author only after mature consideration. But the exhibition of his views would require more space than is consistent with the plan of this little work.

But this doctrine is of too cold and heartless a nature, too repugnant to our natural sympathies, to be readily adopted. It confounds imprudence with depravity, and inflicts the punishment due to moral delinquency on those who have yielded to the strongest, and sometimes the best, impulses of our nature. Accordingly, the policy it recommends has no where been carried into strict execution.

But while such attempts to repress our natural sympathy with human suffering may be equally objectionable and vain, both humanity and a regard to the interests of society require us to lessen the occasions of sympathy as far as practicable. If any feasible plan could be devised to prevent very early and imprudent marriages, the evil would be prevented; but it is apprehended that any legal restraints on marriages beyond those now existing might do more harm than good; and that the poverty which they too often produce cannot be entirely prevented, and admits of but partial remedy.

For those who are able to work but cannot find profitable employment, work-houses should be provided, with the requisite materials and tools, where any healthy man or woman may engage in some useful species of labor, or in those simpler trades which require little or no preparation.

As relief to the poor is often a heavy charge on the community, adequate provision should be made for its payment. The money is more conveniently raised by a direct tax, as by a land or income tax. Aid, however, may be drawn from indirect taxes, laid on whatever contributes to encourage idleness and waste, and to impoverish individuals. Thus, gaming and drinking houses might be made to assist in relieving the evils they had fostered.

But nothing, it must be remembered, is so likely to lessen the number of the poor, as a good system of popular education, good government, and good laws; which cherish individual self-respect, an earnest desire of independence, and an industry free to exercise itself in any way. It is thus that we see the number of poor who are supported by other members of the community smaller in this country than in any other, and that their pressure is most felt in those States in which are the greatest number of immigrants.

CHAPTER XIX.

ROADS AND CANALS.

A LARGE part of the labor of every country, as we have seen, is expended in transporting commodities from the place of production to the place of consumption; and whatever can be saved of this expense is so much added to the net national income. Hence the great benefit of roads and canals. The advantage to the public is shown by the gain to individuals. Thus, suppose that, by reason of the badness of a road, a wagon can transport but twenty barrels of flour one hundred miles in eight days, and that, by improvements of the road, such as making it more level, or firm, or smooth, the same wagon could transport thirty barrels the same distance in four days; the cost of transport would then be reduced to one-third of its previous cost, with more ease to the horses, and less wear and tear of the wagon.

These useful public works are sometimes made at the expense of the State; but it has been found that the public is better accommodated with roads when the right of making them is given by charter to joint-stock companies, who are permitted to charge tolls on the road or canal; so that their cost is in fact paid by those who have the benefit of them.

The advantage of the modern railroad is yet greater, when the articles to be transported are sufficient to repay their great cost. There are only particular situations which are adapted to this species of transportation. These are, first, where there are many persons travelling to and fro, the saving of the traveller's time and expense, enabling them to charge him with a high fare. This is a great source of the profit of railroads on all the great thoroughfares of travel. Secondly, where there is a large and unintermitted supply of a commodity to be transported; as of fossil coal to a city or shipping port, iron, lead, or other mineral, from the mine to its market. Thirdly, for the general transportatation between a populous city of agricultural products on one part, and of foreign or manufactured goods on the other.

In all these cases railroads are most valuable institutions. They benefit both the producing and the consuming classes; they enlarge as well as improve the markets for every species of industry, and yield a fair profit to the capital by which they have been constructed and are maintained.

These obvious advantages, however, have not seldom tempted men to make railroads where they were not wanted, or were premature, and where, consequently, they have occasioned a waste of the national stock. The instances of these improvident undertakings have been so numerous in the United States as to deduct largely from their acknowledged benefits.

The advantage of canals in facilitating the transportation of bulky commodities is yet greater. The far greater quickness of transport by railroads than by canals fits the former for the carrying of valuable merchandise, in which the requisite saving of time is important, as well as in the transportation of persons; but where great expedition is not important, canal transportation is far cheaper. It is commonly reckoned that its cost per mile is from a third to a half of that on railways. One cause of the greater cheapness is that they are kept up at less expense— the first cost of a railroad requiring perpetual renewal, after short terms; another is, that the expense of working them, and the wear and tear of the machinery used on them, is much greater. But, as there must be a large perennial supply of water for a canal, there are only particular situations, corresponding to the natural streams of a country, where canals are practicable. Railroads, however, can be made anywhere, and now impart the benefits of a comparatively cheap transportation to places to which it was formerly denied.

INDEX.

A.

B.

C.

D.

E.

F.

J.

L.

N.

O.

P.

R.

S.

T.

U.

V.

W.

THE END.